M000307317

All the Things That Nobody Told Me:
Finding the Extraordinary in My Journey

by

Charity Pleasant

All rights reserved. This book or any portion thereof may not be reproduced or used in any manner whatsoever without the express written permission of the publisher except for the use of brief quotations in a book review.

Printed in the United States of America.

First Printing, 2021

Copyright © 2021 – Charity Pleasant

ISBN 978-1-7364188-0-2

Special Thanks/Acknowledgments

There are so many words that come to mind when I think about expressing my gratitude for all those who have been a part of this publishing process with me. I wouldn't be here without; God first, followed by my mother and father. I would like to acknowledge my parents for all the love they gave me. I know that I was born in this particular time to serve my purpose. So whenever I get those quite moments to ask myself, what have I done with purpose today? I have to think about how I can allow my journey to impact others in a meaningful way. So, thanks mom and dad, because of you my mind is always thinking about how I can accomplish more of what I'm supposed to.

When I first thought about getting my own words out to share with others about two years ago, I didn't imagine that I would get this far. I'm forever grateful to my proofreader and editor, Stephanie Brennan who agreed to look over my very first draft and gave me thoughtful and priceless feedback. There were several drafts after that first one, each making me feel more confident and excited I was on to something good. I didn't imagine that I would gain such a friend through this process, but she is not only talented at what she does, in addition to paying special attention to detail, but is such a giving person as well. I couldn't appreciate her more.

Table of Contents

Introduction

I've had a love for reading anything that could keep my interests for as long as I can remember. I remember my mother giving me a book called "Black Beauty" as a child and how I read right through it. Nowadays, I enjoy both fiction and non-fiction, focusing on anything that can entertain me for a while or give me knowledge, understanding, or "know-how." Nobody told me that I would be interested in writing a book about my journey. No one told me that it would include laughs and smiles, sadness, and encouragement, as well as become very therapeutic for me. I didn't know I had so many words I needed to say. I felt motivated writing this book because I know that everyone experiences some of the emotions I had, along with a wealth of others, sometimes in life.

I want my thoughts and experiences to be shared with not only the ones I love, also with anyone who is looking for connections, answers, or ideas. I wasn't given a handbook on what to do with my emotions and thoughts or how to absorb and feel them for a moment in time, leave them there, and then move on. I believe my past is meant to be a reflection of memories, not a place to dwell. My journey is not only meant to shape me but help shape others on their way as well.

So, I hope that while you turn these pages that you reflect on your own life and realize that some of these emotions, if not all of them, you will or have already experienced them and know that you are not alone. I hope you experience the same joy reading this book that it gave me writing it. I hope that many will see that this thing called "life" is better described as a journey involving big cycles. It goes around and around, and eventually, we will get to know the patterns, which will better equip us to deal with all life's ups and downs.

Our journeys take us on wild rides that we sometimes don't expect or didn't predict. Even for the most organized planner, there are unexpected hardships that show up in life without warning. These journeys can leave us thrilled, leave us devastated, or leave us healed if we let them. My journey through life looks like so many others at some point or another. I want to connect with you my thoughts, experiences, and joys.

I want to share some of my mistakes too, mistakes that have taught me to grow and align myself with the positive attitude I needed to fully embrace life's journey. You might find while reading this, some similarities or familiarities to your own journey or someone you know. I'm navigating life with my individual compass, finding my way day by day, looking to see my plans line up with my visions. Along the way, I'm finding my extraordinary every day throughout the journey

.

Chapter 1
Humble Beginnings

It must have been a hot summer day on June 9th, 1980, when I burst through the world via C-section at a cool 8 pounds, at Miami Valley Hospital at 11:41 a.m. in Dayton, Ohio. I was my mother's second child of five children, joining my one-and-a-half-year-old sister. My mom was lucky enough not to recall any pain from my birth, thanks to her scheduled C-section birth with me. I had a head full of hair which I would later see braided down or gathered into a huge puff on top of my head as a toddler.

I asked my mom what kind of baby I was. She said I cried and cried for the longest time. Apparently, I didn't let her get much consistent sleep that first six months of my life, switching my days and nights around. She told me it took about six or seven months before I'd sleep through the night. Evidently, my older sister slept all through the night much earlier, mom certainly remembered that. My mom later found out when I was a toddler that I was lactose intolerant. She doesn't know exactly if this was most of the reason I cried so much but thinks that it's definitely a possibility since I ate and drank whatever she did, including milk. My mom consumed many dairy products as she liked to drink milk and eat cheese. My mother said, "one night, I breastfed and put you to bed, and the next morning when I got up to breastfeed, you wouldn't take it." She was

1

engorged, mothers, you know what I mean! She was in pain as well as downright mad at me that I would not latch on. She said that I refused to breastfeed again, and the night before was the last time she ever breastfed me. I had quit just like that cold turkey. She couldn't believe it, explaining she was in tears from the pain of engorgement. She didn't own a breast pump. I was like, "Wow! That's how I rolled my first six months in this world!"

As I mentioned, my sister was about a year and a half when I came home from the hospital. I must've interrupted her world because my mom told me she was a little jealous at first. My mom even told me of a time my sister hit me on the head with a sippy cup while I was just lying on the couch minding my business as a baby. That's okay; I got her back ten times over when I got bigger - just kidding but not really.

We obviously couldn't play together until I was a bit older; eventually, my sister came around. When I was about two years old, and my older sister was four, we both woke up with the Chicken Pox one Christmas morning. It makes sense that we both got it since we played together all the time, being the only children for a while. That must've been a sight for my mother to see! My mother said she always knew when we were coming down with something because we wouldn't eat. That was her sure sign that we were certainly sick. It was just the two of us for about two years until my little brother came home and changed the dynamic duo to a trio. I often can't imagine how my mom or any mother can juggle multiple children in a household while the man is working 40 or more hours per week. I

2

know that money has to be made to support the family, but that leaves a whole lot of expectations and responsibilities on the mother. I sure hope my mom found her moments of serenity and got a few stolen moments of peace every now and again.

One of the earliest memories I have occurred before 1987, the year my mom's mother passed away. Someone was sitting on the couch cutting toenails; who it was, I couldn't remember. But I think it was my dad. I was seven years old or close to it when I heard my Grandmother say, "you shouldn't be leaving those toenail clippings on the carpet, the children will step on them and get hurt." I know she visited us occasionally and brought us things because my mom told me about it. Other than that, I don't have many memories of my mother's mom, except for her beautiful face I see when I think of her. I'd later wonder what kind of "grandma" she would've been had she had the opportunity to spend more time with me. My childhood was filled with so many things that I'd need to write a second book to mention them all. When I sit and look through the pictures of myself taken when I was too little to remember, I think I must've been really loved. There are so many pictures of my siblings and I smiling and playing, sleeping or eating, and just those casual moments that are caught on film. It made me see that those first few years for me were full of love and care in a big world that would impact me as I started my life. It was easy to see that my parents loved me. I was an overall fairly calm toddler, finding toys and things to play with and keep me busy, but boy, I would surely bring my mom challenges in the years to come!

Before I continue into my journey, I want to talk briefly about the two parents that had me. My mom was born in the 1950s in Middletown, Ohio. She had a strict religious mother who raised her and her three sisters. Her relatives and the community had a huge hand in helping raise and guide them. After all, it takes a community to raise a child. My Dad was also born in the 1950s, a little earlier than my mom, but in Tennessee. He was raised with his three sisters and one brother. His family moved around as his father accepted jobs in a few places before settling in Cincinnati, Ohio, for his father's new job.

My parents married in 1977 in Dayton, Ohio, after which is where my story begins. They had two solid years of adjusting to married life before bringing my older sister into the world. She, of course, followed by me, two more brothers appearing in 1982 and 1985, and our baby sister in 1989. So I was brought up in a family of seven (5 children plus mom and dad) in the good ole' days. I call them the good ole days because I didn't really have a care in the world. Whereas kids these days' worry and stress about a lot of things. Rightly so with all of the television shows that aren't wholesome anymore, social media that demean women, glorify violence, and so many other platforms that I didn't have access to growing up. In my days, there were hand-me-down clothes and shoes, none of which I could fit from my sister because she was so much taller than me. We received free or reduced school lunches, had about four television channels, long afternoons playing outdoors, and summers at my Grandparent's house, which was what I considered as vacations. Those are what I call the good ole days because they will forever be in my memories as some of the fondest times I had shared with my family and friends.

My mom tells me that we used to live on Hoover Avenue, even though I don't remember that house. The first house I remember is the single story one on Forest Ave. It was a huge house, big enough for all my siblings and I to have plenty of space and move around comfortably. I remember our two-story home with plenty of room upstairs, all the rooms downstairs could be accessible to each other because you could walk from the living room to the kitchen to the dining area back to the living room in a complete circle. My mom often chased my brothers around this circle with a switch and paused to laugh at the ridiculousness of it. My two brothers were in trouble so often. In those days, my mom would either pick a switch off the tree or grab a belt. I remember being on the end of some of those whippings myself. Most likely, I deserved them.

The house had a spacious backyard for us to play for hours in the summertime. I'm talking we didn't even come in for water because we drank out of the water hose. I'm pretty sure we weren't allowed to come inside on such nice summer days. I don't know what my mom did inside on all those many days of my summer, except for cooking and some cleaning, although it seemed my siblings and I did most of the cleaning. We played hide-n-seek, freeze tag, football, raced each other, and many other made-up games straight from our imaginations. Some days there were so many neighborhood kids in our yard my mom would make them go home. I had so much fun with my siblings and the other children in our huge backyard. I hated when my mom came outside and told the kids we were playing with to go home because it was so embarrassing to me. Some of our made-up games included burying or getting buried by my siblings under a pile of leaves, building things from mud, collecting acorns or pine cones for squirrels, and so many games that seem obsolete today. I could make games up from my imagination and explain them to my other siblings and be laughing for hours.

The neighbors on our right had a small boy and girl our age that I often played with as well. I had to get permission from my parents to leave our backyard and go play with them. Most days, they came into ours because my mom was so over-protective. She didn't like us to go where she didn't have us in her sight. If we were in our own backyard, she could look out the window and see us, but not from the neighbor's yard. Then the most amazing thing happened when I was about ten years old. As close as we were living at the next house to our friends, it got even better. We moved next door to them, literally. They lived in what was called a double or side by side – two families lived on either side of a single property. I didn't know that we were downsizing from a bigger single rental to a smaller rental at the time. A driveway at first separated our properties. What I did know is now my friends, and I shared the same backyard.

We could play together all the time, and I wouldn't even need to ask permission to leave the yard. I made so many new memories of water fights, red rover, and so much laughing and teasing. If anyone told me that I could drive down two city blocks today and not see a single kid outside playing in the summertime, I would not believe them. Apparently, kids today prefer to be indoors playing electronic games or posting on social media platforms instead of interacting with their friends physically. I think they're missing out on so many human social connections to people. My parents and other neighbors helped us solve our arguments and problems while teaching us to play fair with one another. Even those simple lessons go a long way.

There were kids that were always in our backyard playing with us, probably because we were one of the largest families on the block. There were other actions in our backyard as well. Often we'd be in the house at the table eating lunch or dinner, and we'd hear rustling in the backyard only to look outside the window to see police officers chasing someone running through our yard. This happened on several occasions, and I think it scared my mom half to death. Sometimes, it occurred at night and sometimes in the middle of the day. Once, my siblings and I headed out to play, and my younger brothers found a gun in our backyard. He picked it up and ran it up to the back door to my mom; she was horrified. It scared her that it could've been loaded, and he could've accidentally fired it on one of the many children in the yard. She explained that a suspect must've thrown it during a police chase and if we ever saw another one to come get her and not touch it.

Another instance included the same younger brother again, blowing on what he thought was a balloon he found in our yard. On closer inspection, again, my mother horrified and screaming, grabbed it from him and said it was a condom, not a balloon! It wasn't all bad though. We had some really good times celebrating birthdays outdoors, getting sprayed with the water hose, eating popsicles, chasing the ice cream truck, and coming inside when the street lights came on. Every so often, we'd stay outside a little while after the street lights came on while my mom talked and laughed with the adult neighbors on their porches.

Some mornings or mid-afternoons, I walked to the corner store with one dollar and came out with a Chilly Willy to drink, a Little Debbie snack, and maybe a small piece of candy or gum as well. Man, those were the days. I'm not sure if I could purchase one of the three today for one dollar. My favorite Little Debbie snack was Banana Twins, and I loved the fruit punch flavored Chilly Willy with the lemonade one a close second. Whenever the store was out of banana twin singles, I'd grab a Nutty Buddy. Most of what I bought was gone by the time I got back home since I ate it while I was walking. I rarely eat Little Debbie snacks anymore, but I think of my childhood when I see them. Surprisingly enough, growing up, I don't remember having any cavities on my teeth. I brushed at morning and night time, just the recommended twice a day without any problems. Although at times, when my mom thought we ate too many sugary foods, she'd put the whole house on a sugar fast for an entire week. She said she wouldn't be buying any sugary snacks, and we weren't to buy any either. Those sugar fast no doubt helped me once into adulthood to understand how badly too much sugar can affect the body. Thinking at times of how much sugar I'd taken in a particular week, I would just stop eating it altogether for a while, putting myself on a sugar fast. I have often just all of a sudden, and I do mean spontaneously decided to quit some routine to pick something else up totally new. I seem to be able to quit and switch without a moment's notice. It seems when I make up my mind, I just do it. So why is it that over the years into my adulthood, I had eaten so many sugary foods when I knew I needed to cut back? At different times I'd tell myself repeatedly that I need to slow down on eating so much sugar. But for some reason, I only remember quitting cold turkey a few times, never lasting more than a month or two. It isn't that I didn't want to cut sugar out permanently; it's that I haven't disciplined myself enough to follow through. Or is it just all in my head? Sometimes, I find that I can answer a lot of hard questions myself. I found myself at times eating way too many sugary foods than I should've been because there was no real consequence. I didn't gain weight, feel lethargic, or anything after my indulgences. I just knew in the back of my mind that I should've been making a better choice for my teeth as well as my body. I don't know how true my siblings were to sticking to it, but occasionally I still bought sugary snacks at school. It was to my advantage that my mom occasionally removed all the sugar from the house that I didn't get cavities.

My dad took us all on our first real family trip outside the state when we went to New York for our first family vacation. I saw the Statue of Liberty; I rode over what looked like, at 11 years old, gigantic bridges and rode through seemingly never-ending long tunnels. I remember stopping at various gas stations to use the bathroom and gas up our vehicle. My mom cooked fried chicken which we ate cold in the car when we got hungry, along with various snacks we ate on the road. It seemed like it was taking forever to get to our destination. I felt so excited that we were headed out of the state of Ohio as a family for the first time. It proved to be a memorable one too.

We stayed at the Howard-Johnson hotels in Pennsylvania and drove to New York every day. I kept the mini shampoo and conditioner, soap bar, and hotel lotion for many years after as a souvenir. My dad showed us around various landmarks and shared histories with us about them. It seemed as though every time we stopped at a street light, there would be someone who popped out of nowhere and started washing the front window on our eight-passenger van. This scared my mom, of course, but I was surprised that the window washer expected tips without prior approval. I remember my mom cowering down in the front seat each time we drove over a bridge because she was so afraid of water. My mom couldn't swim, and neither could any of my siblings and me. However, I wasn't scared of the bridges, and I laughed at her cringing over a silly bridge. The traffic was so congested, cars were driving bumper to bumper, and I wasn't used to people swerving in and out so closely. That's what made me so nervous. That was nearly 30 years ago. I can't imagine driving in New York traffic today.

Pawpaw

My mother's dad also lived in Dayton, Ohio, while I was growing up. He was born in Middletown, Ohio. We had been calling him "Pawpaw" for as long as I can remember. My mom would drop us off occasionally to spend some time with my pawpaw. There were three familiarities I could count on at Pawpaw's, hearing his police scanner all day, plenty of snacks available, and him chewing on an onion most of the time I visited. I always thought he had the best snacks at his place, like fruit pies, honey buns, and chips. He lived in a high-rise building on the twelfth floor that had both an elevator and staircase.

There would be days I would race with my brothers and sister up every flight of stairs while my mom took the elevator. Some day's mom would make it up there in the elevator before us, but most days, my siblings and I would reach the top of the stairs first. I don't know how we were able to run up twelve flights of stairs, but we laughed and giggled the whole way up. I can't speak for my siblings, but I was out of breath every time we raced up those stairs, and my legs felt like spaghetti by the time I reached the top. I do remember not liking heights, and my Pawpaw had large windows that looked out over the city. I was so scared of being too close to the window because I'd always imagine leaning on it, my weight busting the window out, and falling down twelve stories only to land on the concrete below to my death. That didn't keep me from looking out of it though. I have managed to face my fears quite often. Nobody told me to face them. I just taught myself not to let fear keep me away from seeing or doing things.

Smelling the onion, my Pawpaw almost always had close by gave me a dis-content for them. I had no idea why he always ate them. Sometimes when we visited, he took us downstairs out into the patio gardens with him during the summer months to get fresh air and a break from the television. Several other people outside would always ask him about us, and he'd say, "these are my grandchildren," with pride in his voice. When we got back inside, there were always plenty of sugary snacks and lots of water to drink. He had more than a few dog-shaped banks full of pennies in various areas around his place that he'd let me empty and count sometimes. I never knew why he liked to collect so many pennies since he never seemed to spend them. Or maybe it was the dogs he liked and happened to put pennies in them. Pawpaw was in a wheelchair before I was born, but he never let his wheelchair limit his mobility. I watched him get around from room to room switching from his manual chair to his electrical one efficiently, albeit not quickly. I never realized as a child he had a type of handicap until I was in my teens. Nor did I think about how hard it must've been for him to have had the use of his legs, walking and running up until his twenties. I couldn't imagine the difficulty of being confined to a wheelchair for the rest of my life. I never saw my Pawpaw anything but happy and his laughter was infectious to those around. I appreciate the kind words he gave me as well as the moments he called me out for being wrong. He seemed not to have missed a beat; I knew that I had to straighten up and fly right when he meant business. I adored my pawpaw all the way up until the day he passed away, leaving me with such good memories of how he loved me.

I remember my mom working several odd jobs throughout my childhood. There was babysitting, pressing, and curling people's hair for special occasions, driving a school bus, and a stint at Meijer, only to name a few. She also did fundraisers at our church, baking and selling sweet potato pies, lemon delight, seven up cakes, and bean pies. I always helped her in the kitchen, and I'm sure this is why I like my baked goods today. There was always some fundraiser for usher dues, women's dues, pastor appreciation, or some other sort of thing that needed to be paid at church, and boy, there were a lot of them. This may be part of why she dropped us off with my Pawpaw; maybe she was working, needed a break, or some rest. Either way, I benefited a lot of quality time during those visits. My Pawpaw was extraordinary to me because he always made me feel safe and loved around him, remembered me on birthdays and Christmas every year, and was an overall larger-than-life impact on and in my life.

After my parents separated, my mom took us on another vacation when I was about fifteen or sixteen years old. She drove us to Atlanta, Georgia, where we stayed a few days. We didn't go on many vacations as a family during my childhood, but the two we did linger with fond memories. I did, however, travel out of state with my church in my late teens. In Atlanta, we visited the "Underground," a lively place in the middle of the downtown square. It was full of vendors selling various touristy keepsakes and t-shirts as well as many more souvenirs. I still don't know how my mom managed to save enough to take us on such an extravagant vacation while raising us single-handedly, but I enjoyed myself tremendously.

While in Georgia, we went to Six flags and visited our dad, who moved to Atlanta after being divorced from our mother, and visited a cousin of ours who also lived there. I had such a good time seeing the city and being together as a family. Those two vacations were extra special to me, considering I thought going to my grandparents' home every summer spending a week with my cousins was a vacation. Don't get me wrong, "grandma's house" was extraordinary to me. Although, I never understood why my grandmother didn't look exhausted even once cooking, cleaning, and caring for her grandchildren. She was an amazing lady. My cousins, siblings, and I helped grandma out daily with the chores, although mostly we caused havoc by climbing the apple trees in the backyard or climbing into grandad's boat in the backyard even though he constantly told us to get out of it. When we weren't doing that, we battled each other at ping-pong down in the cool basement or playing some sort of board game.

Although starting my childhood, allergies prevented me from enjoying dairy products. Looking back and considering all of the things I could have and weren't limited to, I'm now more grateful. At the time, I didn't think it was fair that I couldn't eat the ice creams during birthday parties or enjoy the same milk on my cereal as everyone else. My doctor put me on soy products in place of the dairy. So that meant while my brothers and sisters poured milk over their cereal every morning, I had to mix soy powder and water together for mine. As you can imagine, it wasn't very tasty or desired. Besides, I felt left out from what my siblings were having. After a while, I grew used to it because it kept me from feeling sick after consuming regular cow's milk. My mother would let me have pizza with no cheese so as not to feel too left out. I always was given sherbet instead of the ice cream during parties, or other special events, which wasn't a bad deal, especially since all of my relatives and extended family were aware of my dietary needs.

On my birthdays, I would have cake and punch or cake and cookies while everyone else had cake and ice cream. At times I ate the windmill cookies with tears in my eyes from feeling so deprived. But, I must say the consequences I'd experience afterward by having these dairy products when I wasn't supposed to were not worth the trouble. My ears, nose, and throat would swell or close up, and I would get cold or sinus-like symptoms. They would last a few days, so I knew it was better that I didn't have them at all. As I grew older, I started experiencing headaches around twelve years old. I didn't catch on to the fact that they started when I re-introduced dairy back into my diet until my thirties, which may have been the cause of my persistent headache pain. It was because I no longer experienced the same symptoms that I thought I could tolerate. I thought that I grew out of the allergy altogether. If anyone told me that I would be one of the many people who would have to deal with allergies or headaches most of their life, I wouldn't have believed them. I'm trying to suffer through with grace until I can get to the bottom of the cause and keep them at bay.

Thinking back on how my life began, I would not have called my family poor because I always had just enough. Looking back at my friend's vacations, cupboards, and vehicles, I certainly wouldn't say we were rich. No one told me that I would appreciate these early stages of my life that brought me so many valuable lessons like discipline and appreciation. I remember watching my mom writing out a weekly grocery list on such a small budget. It always amazed me how she got so much food with so little money. I'm delighted she let me watch her budget the household money, and because of that, I don't do so bad myself today. She also taught me to automatically put aside ten percent of all that I earned and save a little of every dollar. Reflecting on this life lesson makes me realize as an adult that the rule of giving (or tithing) worked well in her life. No matter how little she had, she always gave ten percent first. That in no way ensured that there was never a lack, but instead, it always provided some sort of blessing. We were treated well, never starved, and always had something to eat. Who could complain about that? There certainly have been people who have been given more challenging beginnings, I'll forever be grateful for mine.

Chapter 2

Contentment

What does it mean to be content? Well, picture this: I'm ten years old, our house is quiet, and it's evening. From room-to-room everything is dark, pitch-black even. I have a bedsheet over my head. It's my turn to find my brothers and sister hiding somewhere throughout our large two story double. I'm laughing while fumbling around, trying not to fall down the stairs, run into any walls, or generally stub my bare feet. I hear voices teasing me, giving me hints in which directions they are hiding. So I turn and quickly move towards the sounds. After what seems like forever, I felt a touch and hear a laugh from a sibling. I still can't see yet but try and tag someone and miss. (more laughter) I feel another tag and turn quickly, laughing and missing again. I know I'm getting close because the laughter is getting louder and louder. A few more steps and... yes, I've got someone. I don't know who it is until I take the sheet off and feel all over the body I've just got. It's my older sister. We all giggled like crazy after I'd tagged the person I found (the three of us, my two younger siblings are too small to play), chatting and telling each other how we were so close to each other and how we got away. It's still dark even though I take the bed sheet off my head because the electricity is off again. One of us pulls out a flashlight and continues to play games with it. This is what the contentment of my childhood looked like. Going without something so basic but not feeling less because of it. I credit my mom and dad in a lot of ways for not letting us feel "poor" but teaching us to make the best out of what we could do versus what we could not. Nobody told me I would use this fond memory of contentment or how it would teach me how to make lemons with my lemonade in the future. I had to see that on my own.

Contentment is, according to the dictionary: "the state of being contented; satisfaction; ease of mind." After our game was over, after we took a turn, it was still dark. This was one of the times the electricity had been turned off growing up from "lack of payment." I didn't find anything abnormal about the lights being off because they had been off before. I was so content with making up games in the dark, giggling and playing ghost, flashlight games, and Lord knows whatever else we made up. Contentment was my state of mind. I had my siblings to make me laugh and play games with. I don't even remember being upset about not having electricity, especially during our games. I had so much space to run around, hide, and make-up spooky games that it didn't feel like a disappointment. Besides, mom put us to bed so early when we were little; there weren't too many dark hours to compete with. Mornings came soon enough, along with the bright sun invading our windows to a brand new day.

Most of my days as a child were just hours and hours of us playing together outside with minimum interruption having a grand ole time. My siblings and I were practically experts in baseball, football, tag, and any other game we made up as kids. I know my mom did an extraordinary job keeping us fed, clothed, and happy. We were only inside on the days that lightning accompanied the rain, otherwise we'd play in the rain as well. I often wonder as an adult how easy it is for children to feel contentment and how adults can learn from them in this way. I have been content many times in my life, but there were times that I wasn't content at all. Such as when I needed more money, more challenge, more responsibility, and the sense of being needed or valued. I find contentment with a few friends around or a lot, and I've been comfortable with no one around at all. As much as I like to socialize with friends and family, I enjoy some alone time too. I haven't always felt that the various jobs I've held had fulfilled me and wanted to get another to achieve that feeling I had been looking for. I have often felt the need to do more in my career, like feeling more useful or leading in a more significant role. I learned from that little game with a sheet in the dark that contentment can be as simple as, *"making do"* with what I have while finding some appreciation in my current conditions. I must continue to see all the opportunities in life and not the limitations. I can be content with a little money in my pocket as well as with a lot of money in my pocket, hundreds of friends, or just a few. What's the difference? The difference is always in my attitude.

When it comes to the way I view an unforeseen circumstance, I have found that a positive attitude makes all the difference in whatever situation I am in. It's because life will keep moving, whether you have a little or a lot, whether you're hungry or full, rather the lights are on or off. My journey will continue whether I'm happy or sad, discontent or very content. I've learned that the more positive

I've kept my attitude rather in times of plenty or not enough; my outlook changed everything. Suddenly, it wasn't so stressful if I couldn't pay a bill on time because I had an opportunity to arrange to pay it late. It didn't have to be a bad day because I spilled my coffee first thing in the morning, along with getting stuck in unexpected traffic because of an accident. When I stop and think, it could've easily been me in the accident; besides, changing my clothes wasn't the worst thing that could happen.

All of a sudden, being late to work doesn't seem like the end of the world. It's easy to have a positive attitude when everything is going great. It hasn't always been easy for me when they aren't, but when I stop to take a good look at my journey with a positive attitude, I start to be grateful. I realize that for every dream un-accomplished, every hope not fulfilled, every wish not granted, that I still have so much to be content about. I realize there's still time to fulfill dreams; it's okay to have hopes and wish that circumstances were different as long as I was acting to change them. I sometimes tell myself, "take a breath; feel my lungs expand and contract." Not everyone has that gift. If there are days I can't run, walk or sit in my local park, look up at the amazing sky, trees blowing in the wind, and birds flying in the air. I'm able to see with the gift of my eyes and hear the hummingbirds with the gift of my ears; someone can't. I read a quote one time that said, "my circumstances don't determine my contentment, but my contentment determines my circumstances." It's an extraordinary thing to be able to find contentment in all life journeys.

Can I borrow an egg?

When I was in my teens, my mother would be gathering ingredients for a recipe in the kitchen like 7-up or lemon delight cake, sweet potato or bean pie, or something else she was working on. She'd start putting the ingredients together only to realize we were short an egg or just a half cup short of sugar to add to the mixture. She'd say, "go next door and ask can you borrow an egg?" Or she'd say, "go next door and borrow a cup of sugar." Our neighbors at the time always gave us that egg or sugar when they had it. Our neighbors did the same, knocking on our door to borrow this or that when all they needed was a little bit to finish whatever dish or Kool-Aid drink they were in the middle of. During that time, we once again lived in a side-by-side (multi-unit), so all we had to do was step over the small porch baluster that separated the two porches. We kept this up all the years we lived at this property. The neighbors had a large family, six or seven kids, so we had a lot in common, often sitting on the front porch conversing small talk with our neighbors. I laughed and got along with one of the girls, especially because we attended the same high school and enrolled in the same cosmetology program. The two of us didn't have a whole lot in common besides the cosmetology program and the fact that we were neighbors, but we exchanged hair tips with one another pretty regularly.

The walls in the double were so thin that I could hear arguments going on next door, so I'm sure that they heard ours as well. I could even hear what our neighbors were watching on television if the volume was up high enough. There were sometimes I'd be down in the basement having conversations with our neighbors through the vents. I know I couldn't have been saying anything of importance though. Other days my siblings or I would open the bathroom window, the house next door would do the same, and we'd be chatting and throwing things back and forth. Those were innocent days when I did all kinds of crazy things to keep myself entertained. My mom always fussed at us for opening the bathroom window. She didn't like when we threw things back and forth to the neighbor's house. Because we always took the screen out of the window, she was afraid we'd fall out. Even though we did drop several items to the ground, we never fell out of the window.

I don't know if many people borrow an egg or a cup of sugar from their neighbors anymore, but I know that I don't borrow from mine. As a matter of fact, I rarely see my neighbors outside at the same time that I'm outside. We come and go at different times because our work schedules are different, I assume. Plus, there isn't really a real sense of community where I currently live. Not many seem to bother each other or go out of the way to get to know one another. Growing up, there was a sense of community. I knew almost everyone's name on the block as well as the others within the household. Today, I probably couldn't name two of my neighbors, and I realize that's sad and partly my fault. Whenever I see this sense of community in any places I visit today, I think it's extraordinary. It amazes me still that with so many cultural differences, people take the time to get to know their neighbors. Not only does it show kindness, but it shows unity, connection, care, and thoughtfulness. When it's trash day, and you notice your neighbor forgot to roll the can down, it's nice that you are willing to bring theirs down to the curb. It's kind when you receive your neighbor's mail and decide to knock on their door and hand-deliver it to them. It's almost unheard of for a neighbor to shovel next door's sidewalk as they're shoveling their own, but I sometimes see it happen in communities. I know because I have done these things for my neighbors in the past. It might not seem a huge deal to you, but it may seem so to someone else. I always try when given the opportunity to show a little bit of kindness, speak or wave, even a simple smile or nod to show my acknowledgment of a passer-by; it could be the only bit of kindness a person gets that day. I believe when I'm content, it shows on my outward facial expressions and demeanor. Nobody told me the key to finding opportunities that would help me learn and grow. When I see those opportunities, I seize them. The contentment of my childhood was possible by the love I felt from my family, friends, and community.

Chapter 3
Organized Religion

Dayton, Ohio, used to be the home base for General Motors, Delphi, Salem Mall, Hara Arena, and many other businesses that thrived throughout my childhood. Whenever I go back to visit now, I'm saddened to see that General Motors has relocated, Hara Arena has been destroyed by a Tornado, and other larger staple places I've mentioned have folded or relocated to other places. This has caused a slowdown in the economic growth for my hometown. But don't count them out. I still see through social media accounts new small start-ups businesses and growth too. The way Dayton looks and feels now is completely different from the eighties and nineties when I grew up. One familiarity is my home church. It still sits in the same spot as it did when I attended grade school and church there all those years ago. It's right at the end of a dead-end street, and it looks mostly the same as it did when I attended before. I only visit occasionally to spend time with my family, for funerals or special occasions. My mom still attends the church regularly, and it will always hold a place in my heart as well.

My mom raised my four siblings and I in church. I say mom because, although Dad attended quite a lot initially, he was not strict with the church rules even though he belonged too. When we were home, my dad didn't necessarily enforce all the rules that were taught by our church, although my mom did. My Dad was an integral part of the print and photography ministry at our church. He worked tirelessly on church programs, directories, photos, weddings, celebrations, and more. My siblings and I were at church so much growing up I'm surprised we didn't have beds there. There was Sunday school, Sunday morning and evening service, Wednesday bible class, Thursday choir rehearsal, Friday saint's meetings, and often other special services in between. We'd stay after many of the services while our Dad was finishing print jobs downstairs in the church basement or the church office for the next service or event. That's where all my friends were, so I got to see them all the time. My sister, brother, and I also attended the church Christian school until I was in the 4th grade. Most of the church members had children that attended the Christian school led by many of the key members of the church, so I saw my teachers and friends all the time. No one told me that a Christian upbringing would lead to such an integral leap into adulthood. I always heard that Christians were set apart, but I wouldn't understand the magnitude of what that meant until far into my adult years. I certainly recommend some sort of spiritual guidance in everyone's life. I don't say that because it was included in mine, but it gives such foundational values that can help a person shape so many ideas and decisions. Because of my upbringing, as an adult, I have a strong foundation with so many values, integrity, and love for people. It wasn't just being taught those foundations throughout my childhood but watching those teachings being lived that helped cement them for me.

A typical Sunday consisted of an all-day affair. Sunday school started at 10 a.m. in which we had various interactive activities that encouraged us to interact with our teachers and one another. Some of the activities were memorizing bible verses or explaining a bible story in front of the class. We normally got a brief 15-minute break before the 11:30 morning service if our Sunday school teacher wasn't long-winded. During this short break, there was a candy shop opened called "The Knick-Knack shop." My sisters and brothers asked me for money to buy snacks after Sunday school about every Sunday that they didn't have their own money. I always seemed to have a few dollars from earning money here or there from styling hair or part-time jobs I often held after school in my teens.

The shop was a little room in the rear of the fellowship hall where there'd be plenty of sugary or salty snacks after morning service. There was a ton of nickel, dime, and quarter candy we could choose from. Some of the items available were: Jolly Ranchers, Lemonheads, Boston Baked Beans, sour candies, soda pop, and sometimes a slice of homemade chocolate cake. Let me talk about this cake that I still remember some twenty years later. The homemade chocolate cake with nuts mixed into the chocolate icing was my absolute favorite. I don't know that I've had a better tasting one to this very day. It had just the perfect balance of moistness and sweetness. The icing was just heavenly. It cost a well spent whopping one dollar per slice, which was one of the most expensive items, but it was worth every penny! Most of the other little candy items I bought weren't for me, but when a friend or acquaintance asked me for it

26

during service. I thought I was kind of cool if I had it to offer, or maybe I thought others would find me cool. Either way, I was more into cake and pastries than candy. To this day, I prefer cakes, cookies, pies, and pastries over any candy or checkout isle sweets. I'm afraid none will compare to the church lady's recipes from my childhood. Although I come pretty close with my other desserts, I bake from scratches like peanut butter cookies or pound cake which are delicious as well.

Once morning service started, it consisted of praise and worship, giving, a couple of selections from the choir, reading an excerpt from the bible, and listening to a sermon. That service usually lasted until about 2 to 2:30 p.m., depending on how the Spirit moved. Sometimes there was an afternoon service at 4:30 in which most of the morning rituals were repeated, and our church might even have an out-of-town guest speaker give the sermon. If there wasn't an afternoon service, we went home, ate dinner, freshened up, and I might even have had time to take a quick nap. If there was, we did everything in a hurry then packed into our car once again to return to church. We almost always had an evening service at 7 p.m. unless the afternoon service ran too far into the evening one. Now, one may think that this is too much "churching," but I enjoyed it because all my friends were attending too. I would sit next to my friends if our moms allowed it. Sometimes my mom said "no" because we would talk too much. Other times I'd promise my mom that I wouldn't talk so much during the service. I also sat in the choir stand with the young adult choir, which sang about once per month. A few times per year, I sat in the rear of the sanctuary with the Jr. usher board. We helped direct people to their seats if they needed to find one, passed out fans and programs, or showed guests where restrooms and other accommodations were.

On a typical Sunday, I had to be presentable, always in a dress or skirt, dress shoes, and sometimes, having to wear a particular color if I was singing in the choir. There was one time of year I was always extra excited and looked forward to, Easter Sunday. It was the only Sunday of the year I got all new clothes from head to toe. My sister and I got our hair hot-combed pressed by our mom, my brothers got their hair cut, and we all were "Vaseline shiny." My mom took us to K-mart for dresses and suits and Payless for shoes. She made sure my sisters and I had frilly and lacy socks and a new pair of church socks for my brothers. No detail was forgotten, down to the lacy hats and gloves for the girls and new ties for the boys. Once we arrived at the church, there were cameras snapping, ooh's and aah's, hugs and kisses, and compliments flying left and right. I felt exceptionally cute on those Easter Sundays. I don't know if anyone was able to focus on the pastor teaching those special days where all the church ladies had their new hats blocking the view of the pulpit. I do believe many people in their new outfits walked up and down the aisle a little more than usual just to be seen in their new outfits. After church, people lingered just a little longer than usual, taking pictures as well as compliments.

Once we got home, there were always Easter baskets full of hard-boiled and dyed eggs and candy that we enjoyed for days. My siblings and I did egg dying the Saturday before Easter and put the baskets together with all the colored grass, although my mom never let us eat anything from them until Easter. I loved to exchange some of my candies with my brothers and sisters for their hard-boiled eggs. They preferred the candy and, of course, thought they were getting a more than fair trade. I remember hating the black jelly beans, or any color for that matter. I wouldn't touch them, although it's funny since I like black licorice today. I always find it odd that I might not like something at times during my childhood, for instance, "peas," but then grow to like it later in adulthood. I didn't see it then, but it must've been tough for my mom to stretch the budget the way she did. She always ensured that we had such memorable Easters every year and looked just as fabulous as any other child at church, even with five kids to purchase items for. We were certainly not the largest family in the church at that time. There were families with seven, eight, nine, or even ten children that belonged to our church family. Big families were not uncommon in the church I grew up. I always assumed one of the reasons was that the pastor taught that birth control methods weren't acceptable. I often heard him say, "the bible says be fruitful and multiply." It seemed to me that those biblical teaching were often encouraged to make church members feel obligated to many children. Nevertheless, I feel special to have had the experiences that I did growing and learning at my church. Easter was definitely a special occasion.

On special occasions, we would have dinner in the fellowship hall immediately after the morning service. I'd leave the service a little early to head down to the kitchen and prep to serve members or guests. I loved helping serve in the kitchen or fellowship hall for meals, especially when we had a guest visit ours church for worship. The diner would precede the afternoon service. I'd be behind the buffet line serving fried chicken or mac and cheese or any other variety of food or dessert. Serving was something I enjoyed doing with a smile, and people appreciated feeling taken care of. I also enjoyed cleaning up the tables after dinner, breaking down the kitchen area, and gathering the trash. Whatever I could do to show I was participating in the need to be filled, I enjoyed. Not everyone enjoys service, but it's something that I have enjoyed for a long time. Serving others in any capacity is rewarding to me because I bring light or joy while making a person feel special. Who knows if that person will feel that feeling of attentiveness the rest of the day? There are some people who live alone. That one act of kindness may be all they see and receive all day. That's why I think it's important to do whatever you do to the best of your ability with enjoyment. If you don't enjoy what you do, it often shows. So if you serve for a living, serve to the best of your abilities. If you're a teacher, go above and beyond what is expected. If you're a leader, lead as if the whole world were dependent on your leadership. If you're an executive, soar to new heights, set new precedents, and don't be afraid to set the bar high. My journey has taught me I'm in this world to stand out, not to blend in. Everyone has a limited time on earth, so I choose to leave the world a little better than when I came into it. Nobody told me that I'd have the urge to do better because I know better. The people who watch me will be the ones taking the lead after I leave this earth, so I want to have set a good example of what kindness and care looks like. I'd like to believe that my religious upbringing has a lot to do with the examples I leave behind.

Sunday was just the start of the week of church for me. As I mentioned, there were many other services and rehearsals throughout the week. Wednesday's bible class wasn't a very long service. It started at 7 p.m. and was generally over by 9 p.m. During Bible class, the pastor would teach from a book of the Bible, an offering would be taken up, and closing prayer concluded the service. Bible class generally wasn't like a question and answer format, but mainly listening and being taught. I brought my own Bible with me most Wednesdays. If I didn't have mine, I'd read off the person next to me as we were all encouraged to witness what it said.

Choir rehearsals also start at 7 p.m. on Thursdays and usually end by 9 p.m. as well. I was in both the youth and the mass choir as an alto singer from my teens until about 19. Being in both choirs along with other church groups kept me busy. I remember helping to coordinate an outreach event with my church youth department. I was tasked to get food donations to help the likelihood of more visitors. I made several calls to local businesses and restaurants and typed a couple of letters to send out. I was so proud that on the day of the event, several businesses donated food to our cause. We had a good amount to share with the local community we connected with through our outreach efforts. The church was grateful, and so was I that businesses in our local community cared to add to our cause to reach people, share the love of God, and our church was able to invite them to our services. It may not seem like an extraordinary thing to some. But when a local church goes beyond its walls and into the community to show love and reveal who they are and why they do it, I see it as ordinary people doing extraordinary things.

I believe I liked church so much because I knew nothing different since that was the way my mom raised me. Friday saint's meeting services were held for members only, starting at 7 p.m. and ending again at 9 p.m. As members of the church, questions could be asked, and feedback would also be allowed on this day. Mostly in the Friday meeting, church business such as finances, rules, and expectations are discussed. These were my childhood religious rituals until I turned about 19 years old when I moved out. Now that I've created my own church schedule, I regularly attend Sunday mornings as my ritual. I still enjoy church today although, some traditions that I followed in my childhood differ from those I follow today. I set aside some of my time volunteering during various church events, church study groups, read my Bible, and pray at home as regularly as I can. Nevertheless, those days growing up are so very memorable because they've created a foundation for me to build my Faith.

Even with all the religious tools and lessons I had growing up, I have often wondered as an adult a few questions. Does God really hear my prayers? Does he really hear me asking him to guide me and lead my path? Has he told me my purpose? Well, I have often pondered these questions, and various forms of answers have come to me through different experiences. I have had thoughts that maybe since I wasn't hearing from him, I was getting punishment for some past sin or something. What I have found is if I really listen, I'll hear the voice of God all the time. He doesn't speak through rumbling in the clouds or a burning bush, but if I listen closely, I can hear his whispers and direction through other wonders like the Bible, inspirational readings or television shows, and even people. All of the questions I had clicked for me one day just as clearly as can be. He spoke clearly to me on a normal day when I was at home once, and I can't imagine forgetting it. Picture this: I was in the kitchen washing dishes at the sink when I heard my son call, "Mom?" I continued to wash the dishes but apparently didn't answer him right away because he repeated, "Mom?" a second time. I continued washing the dishes only to hear him a third time, "Mom?" Follow me with this. I heard him the first time he called my name and the second and the third. He knew I heard him call on me each of the three times. He could've at any time proceeded to tell me what he wanted or needed, except he was waiting for me to answer him.

There was no doubt in my mind that he knew I was listening and had heard him, but he still expected and an answer right away. He didn't once consider that I could wash the dishes and listen to him simultaneously. He wanted my undivided full attention. But what he didn't realize is that I'm constantly listening to him, loving him, working on his behalf all of the time. If he would've just stopped and finished his thoughts, he would've heard my response almost immediately. Only then would he feel more confident that I was listening to his needs. That is extraordinary to me. Nobody has ever told me to think about how God hears us in that way. God doesn't need us to wait until he responds; he needs us to finish our thoughts, desires, and needs. Just bring them before him and watch with belief as he starts to work on our behalf. Even if I don't see God working on my request right away, I can trust that he hears me and is working on my behalf in whatever way he sees fit. So yes, he hears my prayers and is guiding my paths and giving me clarity of purpose.

That's how I should be with God all the time; not just the good but the bad as well. He hears my cries; he hears my concerns and requests or desires. I no longer have to wonder if God is guiding me in my purpose; my belief in him settles that. Whether I hear him answer right away or not, I can be confident he hears me, and you can too. Once I take a problem to him, I can be certain that I can leave it there and trust he's working it out. There's no reason to stress or worry over something when I can trust those things to God. Just as my son knows I hear him speaking to me, I'm confident that my Godly Father hears me speaking to him. I can't remember if I eventually answered my son or just turned around and looked at him, but he finally told me what he needed to tell me. Experience has taught me not to wait until I hear God answers; I should just talk to him, knowing he's listening while letting him guide my steps. I believe God gives us his attention all the time, which should satisfy our needs. It's extraordinary how a small instance like this was used to explain to me the spiritual but extraordinary nonetheless.

I hope that you are encouraged that no matter how hard the situation may be, and I know at times it feels impossible. You can rely on God to listen and hear your prayers. Through loss, grief, bad relationships, impossible finances, hunger, fear, frustration, and any other thing that life may throw your way. Try God. Lord knows we try everything else. At times the enemy allows people to live a life without hardship, so they don't turn to God. So if you're comparing your hardships to someone who seems to never have any hardships at all, be thankful. Our struggles are what turn our hearts to God. Without them, we wouldn't know who he is or what he is capable of doing. I recommend you use reason, logic, and understanding when facing your hardships. Above all, try God. Even if you currently live a life without hardship, take a few minutes each day to thank and acknowledge him. Don't let the enemy keep you from having a relationship with him if it's hard to determine whether you should keep pushing through hardship when circumstances seem to put a roadblock up at every turn. Try listening.

Sometimes, it's difficult to tell whether or not the block is a sign that we shouldn't go in that direction. Or it could be a test to see how much we want to accomplish the goal. One way that I try to differentiate between the two is to write down all the risks of the lesson (also known as failure, I call it a lesson) if I don't succeed. How much will those lessons cost me? Can I afford the costs? I'm not just talking tangible ones but mental and time costs too. Is what I'm trying to accomplish lining up with my purpose in life? If it does, I keep persevering through. You may be able to ask yourself several questions that may enlighten you to move or not move toward what you think maybe a good plan. This type of thinking helps me with major decisions I face. No one has ever told me to think this way when approaching a major decision. I'd like to think it's an extraordinary feeling to be able to look beyond ordinary approaches to life answers to operate outside the social normality's.

Chapter 4
An Education

My Christian school days started out for me in kindergarten with teachers I already knew because they all attended my church. My days were filled with Bible lessons, reading, math, social studies, science, and all the other extras like art and gym. I learned how to sew and knit in art class and enjoyed playing red rover and kickball in the gym. I was taught to be honest, respectful, obedient, and hardworking. Nowadays, paddling is practically gone, but yes, it was allowed when I attended school in the 1980s. I only remember being paddled once in the five years I attended the Christian school. I have no recollection of what I did to warrant the said paddling, but I'm sure that I deserved it. I remember learning being very fun and getting good grades, mostly all A's. I also had to attend a weekly bible study during school hours where we all gathered together for a bible lesson and prayer. We also pledged allegiance to the American and Christian flag during morning assemblies. Most, if not all, of the rituals, are no longer carried out in any public schools in these modern times; perhaps it is in a private school setting. Those incremental foundations stuck with me throughout my life. I have remembered the lessons I learned, whether they came through a lecture after I did something wrong or was just being called out for the visible bad decisions I was making. I have tried to live by the values and disciplines I was taught at my workplaces, in relationships, and with countless decisions made over the years. I cannot say that I was always successful at it, but I have indeed tried to improve daily.

There was a time during the 3rd grade I had an allergic reaction to some dairy products I had gotten into. My mother wrote me a note to take to school the next day to let my teachers know I would have a few reactions, including having a hard time hearing because my ears, nose, or throat generally closed up. That day at school, I heard my teacher calling my name, but I pretended not to hear it. I took advantage of the fact that my mom made them aware of my hearing not being at its full capacity. I let my teacher call on me a few more times that day before I answered, feigning that I hadn't heard her the first time she called. I must've wanted a little extra attention and sympathy that day. Even though I got plenty of attention both at home and at school regularly, for some reason, I wanted more. I wasn't the sort of person that normally liked to be put on the spot but preferred to be pulled aside individually or privately. That year in third grade, I must've wanted that individual pity or attention to quietly let others know what I was experiencing as my norm, giving an up-close look into what my allergic reactions were like.

During my fourth grade year, I switched from my Christian setting to public schools. Between grades four and six, I attended Webster elementary in Dayton, Ohio, until I advanced to the seventh grade. I remember my first few days being so shocking because of the difference in atmosphere. Kids were talking back to teachers, cursing at each other, physically fighting, getting suspended, and overall behaving so poorly in a way that I was unaccustomed to seeing. I know now that I was sheltered throughout my first few years being in a private school. This was the first time I realized life was so much bigger than the bubble I lived in. Some people ever only live in their neighborhood for most of their lives. Some may travel in the same circles of people, groups, and places, not knowing how things may look from a different viewpoint. It still surprises me that some may never travel outside their city, state, or country to see all the thousands of other cultures in our world, see different living conditions, or appreciate earth's beauty. The world then seemed much bigger than my little pocket in which I lived. I found that if I only expose myself to what I'm comfortable in, then I won't have a clue of what others experience or what the rest of the world is really like. It's hard to have empathy with people when you haven't walked a mile in their shoes.

My home life exposed me to things in my neighborhood like adult prostitutes, drug transactions, and police chases. Later, I saw all types of interactions between kids at my new school: demeaning, bullying, and plain mean. Fortunately, I managed to keep making the right decisions and keep good grades throughout my elementary years. It had a lot to do with having good teachers. Like my fourth grade teacher, who was kind to me and made me feel welcomed during my transition. She was memorable to me because I liked her sweet demeanor, and she seemed to love teaching. My fifth-grade teacher was a no-nonsense teacher who didn't play in the classroom. I remember her looking over the rim of her glasses, checking over my shoulder and others as she paced around the classroom. Nobody told me that the sum of all my teachers, both private and the public would shape how I looked at teachers today. I expect teachers to be strong yet understanding, friendly yet disciplinary, and supportive but demanding that all students give their best efforts. These were the attributes that helped shape me throughout my early learning years.

All things said, I pretty much soared through my elementary years, watching and observing other kid's actions, listening to my teachers doing what I was supposed to do. Because I had strict training when I was a child, I didn't get caught up or tangled in what others around me were doing in my new school setting. It felt like an eye opener but yet not tempting for me to join what everyone else was doing when I switched from Christian to public schools. Not every student was exhibiting poor behavior; there were many awesome ones who carried themselves well. I just wasn't used to any child that didn't respect adult authorities. During 4th, 5th, and 6th grades, I made a few friends, generally got along with most of the kids I was around and remained mostly quiet and observant those years. All my teachers said I was a good student because I was so well-behaved. Moving from a small Christian school to a larger public one really introduced me to a lot of thoughts and ideas I may not have otherwise been introduced to, for instance, Darwinism, Evolution, or even sexual health. I don't know that I would've been exposed to worldviews not backed by religion. Plus, the sheer increase in the number of students to me was crazy coming from a school of less than 100 going to one with about 400 students and staff members.

During elementary, I tried my hand at sports, running shorter distances like a 40-yard dash or a relay race around the track. I thought it would be something I'd be interested in. Turns out, when it came to sports, it wasn't my thing, but I was pretty good at other scholastic events in elementary. During my fourth grade year, I won second place at a school-wide speech contest. I still remember the poem I recited, "What is America to me?" I'd gotten student of the month, honor roll, entered spelling bees, and received student achievement awards. I was involved with the school band playing the flute in elementary school too.

Even with all of the awards and recognitions, I was being talked about or teased by kids who thought I was strange or dressed funny because I only wore skirts to school. All the girls wore skirts at my Christian school, so it had never been an issue until then. Although the teasing wasn't a nice feeling, I persevered through it, all the while I was making good grades. To complicate things a little, I was being chased home by a boy who had a crush on me. I used to take off running as soon as I got off the bus, hearing the kids on the bus cheering me on, and hearing the boy close behind me catching up. In that matter, boys wanted to be around me a lot more than the girls did. From what I observed, the popular girls talked about less popular ones for no reason. Tearing down their clothes or shoes, hair or looks, and just assuming that others were "stuck up." Light-skinned girls would say mean things about dark-skinned girls or the reverse. It didn't really seem to matter how someone looked, even at the elementary level. You were generally talked about unless you were the popular one, which I wasn't. That didn't keep me from being able to stay true to myself and to my few true friends. The teachers loved that I was such a respectful student and never gave them any trouble. They let my parents know every year during those parent conferences or notes added to my report cards. Public schools broadened my thinking when it came to the realization that not everyone was taught the same foundations I had. If it weren't for the confidence and ability to be strong in my character, I could've easily fallen through the cracks. Nobody told me that I would have to stay focused on making the best of the adjustment, but I did. I don't remember my parents asking me how was school when I came home each day. I guess they assumed I adjusted well since I always came home in a good mood. I went from knowing everyone in my Christian school to not knowing anybody in my new public school. Still, I eventually found my footing and adjusted well to my new environment.

I breezed into Fairview middle school in Dayton, Ohio, with all my teachers raving to my mom about how I was such a good student, only I wasn't always so pleasant at home. My teenage years were filled with plenty of attitudes, mean looks to my mom, talking back, and outright disrespectful at times. My mom and I had a rough patch during these years, often not agreeing or seeing eye to eye on any of her rules. I know now that I inherited this trait from my dad, which I believe to be part of the problems that occurred between my mom and I. I was so much like him, and I think that probably bothered her on some levels.

Although my elementary years went by mostly positively and successfully, middle school was a little more difficult for me because kids were more openly mean and opinionated. I didn't endure much teasing in elementary, but it increased a little in middle school. I ignored it all, went to work part-time after school, completed my homework, and helped out around the house with chores when I got home. My first real tax-deducting job at fourteen years old was as a custodial assistant at the Roosevelt Recreation Center in Dayton. My duties were to help the head custodian empty wastebaskets from offices, cubicles, restroom trashcans, refill toilet paper and hand towels, mop floors, vacuum carpets, clean commodes, etc. anything else that was needed to enhance and refresh the building. I remember liking my first job very much and enjoying the lady that I worked with. As the head custodian, she taught me to work as though the CEO was watching me or I was preparing the areas for one of my friends or family. She always told me to clean as though I were cleaning for them. If it was important to me for them to have a clean and sanitized area, I should work just as hard to make it the same for others.

I remember having two really good female friends at school during my seventh and eighth-grade years. I will call them "Dainty D" and "Diva S." We all were different in our own rights. Dainty D was what I'd call super smart, very soft-spoken, and a straight-A student. Diva S was so confident, could be very witty, especially when she rolled her eyes, and always walked with her head held high. Then there was me, the slightly shy one who got average grades, did what was expected of me, and very much enjoyed the company of the other two. We shared some classes and the same lunch period. The three of us all played the clarinet in the school band. I didn't feel like a natural but practiced at home a lot and was pretty good after switching from the flute I played previously. I remember putting on various shows for the school and parent audiences. I would record myself at home practicing and playing various tunes. I always thought it amazing that Diva S had so much confidence no matter what others said about her, we were alike in that way. She never let other kids slow her stride or rock her confidence. Other than band, my friends, working a part-time job, church, and the activities that went on there were what occupied most of my time during middle school.

I continued to stay involved at my church throughout my seventh and eighth-grade years. I was involved in things like teacher assistant in Vacation bible school, singing in the youth and mass choirs, and served on the Jr. usher board, greeting and directing people to their seats during services. Service stayed a priority for me during my middle and high school years. I always remember being happy as I did these different ministries. I supposed that was part of being a Christian; loving and serving people. I don't know why I didn't invite more friends or acquaintances that I knew to church, other than I already had so many friends who attended the same church already. Also, I imagine I was somewhat ashamed to share my religion because it wasn't flattering how I dressed and all the rules I had to follow. I didn't think anyone wanted part of that. I felt particularly confident one day when I invited Dainty D to church one

Sunday, and she agreed to come with me. Dainty D must've been touched by whatever the pastor was teaching about that Sunday because when I looked over, tears were streaming down her cheeks. I asked her after the service if she had any questions about my church, but she said no. I thanked her for coming as my mom dropped her off, never asking her about her emotional experience during the service. She didn't attend with me again, but we remained friends throughout our time together during middle school.

I remember middle school being more challenging because kids talked a lot about what other kids were wearing. I, again at the time, was wearing skirts only, even in the winter seasons, so I was an open target for the kids who liked to pick on others. My peers couldn't fathom why I wasn't wearing pants in the winter to stay warm. I'd always tell them, "It's because of my religion." It was technically the rules of the church that I grew up in. In hindsight, I know now I should've let it be known that it was a conscious choice that I was making each day to dress how I did. Well, more of my mom's choice since I had to follow the rules she had in place at home. I didn't always agree with the rules she had in place and fought her tooth and nail on following them. She always wanted my skirts below my knees, or the split in the back could only be a tiny one, so we were constantly fighting about my wardrobe both for school and church. I thought my church had the rule of no pants for women as an expression of being and looking feminine. I couldn't ever remember a time where our church didn't have a say in how we dressed. I couldn't understand how they thought their rules correlated to the Bible, but my mother insisted on enforcing that and other rules all year round. I had options like leg warmers, tights, or long coats, none of which I was interested in wearing.

I knew several females from my church wore pants in the winter to stay warm, only my mother didn't allow us to do so. Mom stuck to our religious rules in or out of church very strictly. I didn't understand why she felt so committed to letting a minister at church affect how she raised and cared for me. I fought and argued with her about wearing stockings in the summer, staying out late, and wearing makeup. I won some arguments, but she probably a lot more. The things I learned in the end, which nobody told me, would help me tremendously to respect authority. Not only did these learning curves help me to respect authority, but also to conform when it's needed and stand up when I disagree on things. It taught me to change my surroundings when they're not conducive to what I want and need in my life. I don't know if many children these days are taught to be respectful to adults and authority figures from what I've experienced. I find out now that children are mimicking the same disrespectful nature that they see their parents portray. The models or examples that children have in their home life just aren't the same as I had growing up. Sometimes parents don't enforce respecting adults or authority figures, or maybe both parents and children have chosen to conform to the social cues of doing and saying whatever feels good. Whatever the shortcoming was and still is, I hope we can bridge the gap between our generations.

At the end of my 8th-grade year, my middle school went on a field trip to Kings Island. I was looking forward to this field trip for weeks. It was the end of the year and was a treat for me, having put in all the work needed to move on to high school. I got to hang out with two of my best friends and couldn't wait to ride roller coasters, eat amusement park food, and go to the water park. The day was going well. We were about halfway through the time we knew we had to report back to the bus. So, we made a point to head to the waterside of the amusement park so that we could have a little time to dry off before going back to the bus. So off we went to the locker rooms to change and lock up our belongings. We slid down slides with our donuts, took rides that promised to get us soaked, and giggled and played the whole way through. We stood on the bridge where we knew we would get soaked by the water splashing from the water ride below. The park was so crowded, and all of the water rides had long lines.

I don't remember what this particular ride was called but, I walked up at least a couple of dozen stairs to get to the top of this adventurous-looking water slide for what seemed like miles to get to the top. This one didn't have a donut with it, so I didn't have anything to make me feel secure about the slide down at all. I was so nervous because, first of all, I was not too fond of heights, but more importantly, I didn't know how to swim nor the depth of the water below. I didn't tell my two friends, Dainty D or Diva S, that little detail because I was a little too embarrassed. My mother never let us swim or put us into lessons when we were younger. It was because of that that I had a small fear of the deep water. Even though I knew this slide didn't have a donut to keep me safe, I just sat my body at the top of the slide, and off I went.

I would soon find out how deep the water was at the bottom. I was so scared going down those curves, not knowing when I'd hit the water. There were so many twists and turns that a person who swam would've enjoyed it enormously. At some point, I closed my eyes because I was afraid I would slip up over the edge, fall off the slide, hit the concrete, and die. The next thing I remember is hitting the water and sinking directly to the bottom of the pool. I must've been down there for longer than I should've because someone (lifeguard) grabbed me and pulled me back above the water and out onto the edge of the pool. I thought to myself, okay, I almost died, and two, what in the world was I thinking? The lifeguard afterward was fussing at me about almost drowning and the dangers of getting into deep water without proper experience. Needless to say, my friends were pretty concerned, but supportive too. I don't know why I didn't come clean before we headed up the stairs to the slide. They were my two best friends and would've understood if I'd just waited for them at the side of the pool.

When I became an adult, sometime in my twenties, I paid for my very first swim lessons. I have gotten in the pool again many times since my eighth-grade year. The difference was I was a lot more sensible about it, not going in water deeper than I could stand up in. After I'd gotten through a few sessions of swim classes, I'd gotten comfortable enough to get into water five feet or under. After all, I was 5'6", so I could stand in the water and float quite nicely by then. The near-drowning taught me a few things. One, to always be true to myself and my friends. No matter the opinions others may think of what I can or cannot do, always be truthful about it. Two, whenever I'm willing to take a risk, I have to accept that things may not turn out in my favor. This taught me to have better management of the risks that I take in life, have a plan B, decide whether the risk is bigger than the reward, or gain more knowledge so that the risk is not a risk. I never told my mom about this event because I knew she wouldn't be happy about it. Because my mom had such a fear of water not being able to swim herself, I would go through my entire childhood without knowing how to swim. Even with all the drama I caused that day at Kings Island, it was a fun and memorable trip to close the end of my time in middle school. I'll always remember that I can trust true and supportive friends with my vulnerabilities and shortcomings.

High School

I took on that attitude of risk management as I started my freshman year of high school at Patterson Co-op Dayton, Ohio. Patterson was a high school that included a career center where certification could be earned in several different fields upon graduation day. The three years I spent in high school was a mix of difficult and fun times. I had no idea as a freshman that I'd be graduating a year early.

I not only started at the bottom of the social chain but continued to be noticeably set apart with my skirts worn every day, no pierced ears, and still quiet demeanor. I was beginning to open up more that year, becoming more of a people person. Every time I changed schools, what fascinated me was the difference in personalities each teacher and student had. I loved observing people and their behaviors by this point. I thought I had decent looks and the boys seemed to like my long hair and pretty smile. Although they did little else but talk to me because I kept them at bay. I wasn't like some of the other girls who seemed to be promiscuous by the way they openly talked about it to each other. Not all the girls were as easy-going and open to meaningful conversation as I was.

Some of the girl students frowned and asked about the skirts I wore daily or how I styled my hair. I changed my hair a lot because I was planning on entering the Cosmetology program during high school. I was always fascinated about what I could do with my hair, styling it in different shapes and patterns. I went through a rough patch during freshman year when I had almost all my hair cut off, down to about two inches all over with a section of long hair at the nape of my neck. (AKA joe dirt look) My hair looked good the first week I had it cut because the stylist that did it for me was good at short hair. Until then, my hair was below shoulder length practically my whole life, and I had no idea how to style my short hair daily. I knew that if I wanted my hair to grow back, I shouldn't hot curl it every day with an iron. So, most nights, I would put a few hair rollers in the top and slick the side parts back into a banana clip in the morning and head off to school. I have to admit it did look pretty bad, which led to a lot of teasing in the first part of freshman year. But the boys never seemed to notice or care, which made me wonder why some girls were always so critical about things that seemed not to be a factor for them.

It was because of the combination of teasing, me continuing to get by with average grades, and not having a parent at the house in the morning to wake me up that got me off to a bad start freshman year. With no one to ensure I got off to school that year, I missed about 30 days of school freshman year, maybe more. My parents were divorced, and my mother worked early mornings. She relied on me to get myself up and to school, and I was old enough to do so, but that didn't always happen. Meanwhile, my two good friends from middle school went to other high schools, so gone was my support system. I had to work on making new friends the first year which was hard because I was particular about choosing high-quality friends. I, at least, recognized a few other students from middle school that year, so I didn't feel completely alone. Although I had a friend or two, it was just a whole different dynamic for me to get adjusted to. The coursework wasn't difficult aside from the math, which no one at home could help me with. The teachers weren't terrible either. I just kind of felt like I was in a box by myself with no one else who connected with me the way I wanted.

Also, I was allowed to make up some of my missing work, so my grades weren't horrible. One or two afternoons home on the city bus, upper-class girls would throw things like balled up paper on the bus, a few times landing in my seat. It didn't happen much, and I never even saw who threw the paper but knew who the bus bullies were. The few times that happened, I quietly ignored it.

One day, I turned around and said something, probably to no avail. However, I was determined not to let it get me down because I knew I only had to be with these kids long enough to finish high school. I knew once I finished high school, I would probably never see or interact with any of these kids. So why bother getting any emotions fired up when I already had long-term plans for my life, and my plans didn't include any of them.

Nevertheless, I wouldn't have missed so many days my freshman year of high school if I wasn't avoiding the mean kids, being a little less confident, over-sleeping, or just plainly not motivated to go. It was relatively easy for me to catch up on most of the work I missed. So I sailed through that year, making average grades again, putting forth little effort in any of my classes, but still passing them all.

There were good days' freshman year, like spending my bus fare home in the school cafeteria to enjoy a warm frosted honey bun with my lunch or donuts and orange juice for breakfast. I remember it being so worth it even on those hot days walking home since I'd spent my bus fare. I walked so fast that most days, the bus driver would pass me about a block or two away from where I'd normally get off. I could hear the kids through the open windows in amazement, yelling, "dang, she walks fast." I don't remember telling my mom I used my bus fare often for a sweet snack in the cafeteria. But boy, I enjoyed every little bite! I also enjoyed several subjects at school like Science and Social Studies. There were days in English the teacher would put on a movie like *"To Kill a Mockingbird"* instead of lecture and classwork. Those movie days were particularly relaxing if I didn't fall asleep. *"To Kill a Mockingbird"* was filmed in black & white, which I loved, but I knew I had to pay attention to it as well as other movies because we had to complete reports on them afterward. I enjoyed Social Studies because I learned so much interesting history. To this day, I enjoy informative subjects and documentaries. It's interesting to me to be able to tie the present with past histories.

My sophomore and junior years went by mostly pleasantly because I joined the Cosmetology program. In that program, I couldn't miss school as I had done in my freshman year because my hours were tracked and recorded for state board certification. The teasing also eased up quite a bit because kids saw that I refused to be bothered by it. I guess they expected me to cry, react, or fight them because of it, but I didn't. I never went home crying to my mom about it because I didn't care about the words that came out of students' mouths. During my sophomore year, I brought home my mannequin head regularly, which I was practicing styles and cuts on during my Cosmetology classes. The kids on the bus started admiring and complimenting the styles that I was creating. I enjoyed my sophomore year a lot better and didn't miss nearly as many days as I did my freshman year. Plus, I had a phenomenal Cosmetology instructor I really liked. My Cos instructor always had kind words for me even though she was a no nonsense lady.

Skip to the middle of my junior year, my cosmetology instructor called me into her office sometime during my second quarter, she made me aware that I'd worked so hard to meet all of my high school requirements that I could graduate a year ahead of my class. She told me all I needed to do is take one semester of twelfth grade English, and I could graduate. So I talked with the high school counselor and enrolled in the Senior English class the following quarter. I went home to tell my mom, and she was on board with my new plans. I was elated to be leaving high school a lot sooner than I originally planned. Turns out I would be graduating with the few upperclassmen that gave me grief earlier. Funny how life works out sometimes. Haters can be consumed with trying to intimidate people, but I wasn't insecure. So, it didn't stop me from persevering through high school without being scathed, ending up on the same level playing field, or passing them by. I didn't feel the need to attend my junior prom since I was so close to graduating high school, so I didn't. With the junior year being my last year of high school, I was just excited to get up out of there and start my life as an adult. I couldn't wait to see where life would take me, and boy has it been a ride.

Reflecting on my education helped me realize how much I enjoyed my childhood regardless of not doing certain activities. I had people around that loved and cherished me. Now that I'm an adult, if I disagree with organizational policies or values that cannot be changed or revised, I remove myself from that organization (church, job, social groups, etc.) There are so many different options available today; therefore, a good fit for everyone is attainable. I never let a few bad experiences keep me from participating in an organization. There's not much I would change, and I hope a lot of others can say the same about their education as well. Nobody told me education throughout my school journey would include not only the teachers but the students too. I learned what I didn't want to become; rude, mean, belittling, or anything that could make another person feel less. It's extraordinary to have been able to learn more than the school curriculum and life lessons to live by.

If anyone told me that these memories would have me smiling as I typed away, I would've started gathering these memories long ago. The summation of my school environment taught me that people would sometimes talk about you, make fun of you, or otherwise make you think you don't belong. Furthermore, in life, you have to learn from the people and experiences you have. After all, it gave me "thick skin." If I would've shuddered, cowered down, and cried every time folks said an unkind thing, I would've been sad too many times. I learned that I wasn't what people thought of me, and I didn't need to prove that I wasn't what they said of me.

All I had to do was live my life, and the proof was in my actions. I learned that I didn't need to be liked by everybody or blend in. It's ok to stand out. I already was surrounded by many people who loved and cared for me. So I walked with my held high right through my haters. I never once let them see me sulking because I knew they didn't understand me or where I planned on going with my life. Nobody ever told me that children would be committing suicide years later because of bullies in horrible numbers. No one certainly told me that the very thing would hit so close to home, affecting my friends and acquaintances' children. I only pray that parents help their children realize that words and actions are powerful. What we do today can either hurt or help someone tomorrow. Not every person is as resilient and strong as I was or had the same level of emotional support needed. My true friends were my rocks. My church family and neighbors held me accountable. Today there are so many resources available for those who need to work through their feelings. Loving yourself as I did will go a long way. People will only see what they see. What they saw at my graduation was me walking across the stage full of confidence and relief, receiving my diploma proudly with the ones who loved me from the beginning, screaming my name from the crowd.

Chapter 5

Ode to my Alma mater

After I graduated high school in 1998, I stayed home and worked for one year. Along with starting a part-time job at a church member's beauty salon, I picked up a job or two here or there to supplement my client base. I held the two jobs right before college as a banquet server at the Holiday Inn hotel and a server at Steak-N-Shake restaurant, not simultaneously. I mostly enjoyed working various hours as a banquet server because I met all kinds of people, ate all kinds of foods, and learned etiquette for weddings, board meetings, and more. The hours at the hotel varied between mornings and evenings, depending on the event. I liked serving at Steak-N-Shake because it gave me the kind of cash I could spend daily, and besides, I was meeting new people every day. I was good at handling several tables and even had requests from people to sit in my section. At the time, I wasn't thinking about saving money for college because I'd planned to support myself with my cosmetology license.

The thought of going to college never crossed my mind because my parents didn't push it. Plus, I had always planned on being a Cosmetologist after high school, earning my license shortly after graduation. However, it wasn't easy to make the big money as I had thought. It took time to build a client base. As young as I was, I wanted to make money with little effort so I could spend it having fun with my friends. My best friend at the time talked me into applying for the same college she was going to, Miami University, Middletown, so I did, and we both got accepted. I have to admit I was excited about leaving home for the first time.

We went off to school together just about 30 or 45 minutes from Dayton to the Middletown, Ohio campus. The campus wasn't huge though it had more than a few buildings and had a nice layout with well-maintained grounds. I was impressed by what Miami of Ohio had to offer, and it seemed to have this close-knit kind of community feel. So, I decided I was leaving home, doing so with my best friend, who would become my roommate in our off-campus apartment. My mom helped me find furniture that worked well in my first apartment, and my best friend and I were having a blast with both of us living away from home for the first time.

My freshman year of college was completely different from high school. People could care less about what others were wearing or how their hair looked. Although, I kept myself up a lot better and made a conscious effort to look presentable. I attended a few parties, held down a part-time retail job, and managed to make the dean's list both semesters. I made friends easily; boys actually wanted to date me and weren't shy about asking either. I took all my pre-requisites while enjoying my new found independence. I was really happy that I didn't gain the freshmen fifteen everyone told me about. I do believe that advantage had directly come from my high metabolism.

I picked up a book called *"Rich Dad Poor Dad"* during college at my local library. I knew by the time I finished, it was more than a good read – it was an education too. I knew then and there, I had to read anything and everything this author had to offer because of the rich lessons I took away. The book was just as meaningful to me as the other parts of my college education. Robert Kiyosaki has written about over 16 books, including some co-written ones. Over the years after college, I have gotten a hold of all of them, diving in with excitement to what I would learn and use. All of the books have insightful information on real estate or business. All are great reads for entrepreneurs in my opinion.

For the small number of people who haven't read or heard of the book, "Rich Dad Poor Dad" chronicles a boy growing up spending a lot of time with his friend's dad, a businessman (rich dad). He loved and spent time with his biological father but connected more with his rich dad's practices. His biological father was successful in his own right, spending his career working as an employee. The book explains how his friends' rich dad earns money (making money work for him) compared to his biological dad working extremely long hours to earn money. I don't want to give the whole thing away, but I recommend reading this book even if you're not interested in business. The book clicked on the light bulb for me. Don't get me wrong, I'm not knocking anyone who works their 9 to 5's and loves their jobs. There are quite a number of people who are good at their job, find their work very satisfying, and make a lot of money doing what they do. I'm thinking in terms of hitting the glass ceilings, tired of working long hours, and craving to manage your earning potential, work schedules, and career direction like me.

I started reading many motivational books and listening to them on cassette tapes or CDs in my car before and during my college years. The tapes always passed the time for me when I was back and forth between work, school, and other places. And if I tell you this book changed my life, it's an understatement. I hadn't, before, Rich Dad, heard of such thinking described in it, not even in my college courses. The author had me re-thinking my thought process on how to become financially secure. He explained so clearly the methods he used in great detail. As soon as I finished his first book, I knew I wanted to learn more about him and his business practices. I couldn't get it out of my head how the author took intentional steps to craft the life he wanted and teach others as well. He wanted to show other people exactly how he did it. I was confounded about the authors' willingness to share his formula for success in great detail without leaving out any of the failures. I found it extraordinary that he wanted to share because some people who become successful don't want to disclose their formulas for fear of losing their margins of success. Here, the author of the book helps his fellow man or women to achieve success as well.

I found I was pretty good at living on my own, budgeting bills, and prioritizing my time. I had decided to major in business management because I already had a cosmetology license and wanted to gain practical knowledge of the business side. The courses like accounting, marketing, business law, finance, Microsoft office, and so on were invaluable tools for my business launch years later. I was diving into my core classes and rooming with my best friend; college was going pretty well. We had few disagreements while sharing a space and were able to talk about them and move on fairly quickly when we did. I had gotten to know my way around the relatively small campus and was good friends with my guidance counselor and mentor. I also had a solid group of close-knit friends to add to my best friend and inner circle. My roommate and I cooked a lot, and word got around campus that we were "throwing down" in the kitchen. That connected us with a few people who liked to break bread with us quite frequently, and I liked the socialization. I managed to keep a decrease in sugary sweets for a while. It's because I've made up in my mind that I want good health long term. Plus, I did a little research on what too much sugar does to the body from the inside. So making healthier food choices during my college years was a no-brainer for me. We went to a few parties, campus social activities and had a good time, all the while maintaining good grades. Every time I chipped away at a goals like, passing my classes, the progress I made pushed me, that much closer to my degree. Rather it was passing a final exam or turning in a paper by its due date. It was all an accomplishment for me.

During the second year of college at Miami of Ohio, I attended a church in Cincinnati located off of Reading Road. I was new to the church and loved that it was full of young people my age. Since I was in my early twenties, it was a perfect fit for what I was used to at my home church in Dayton, Ohio. After seeing my beliefs in line with what the church was teaching, I immediately joined. I got involved with the youth choir and started hanging out with some young adults outside of services doing things like group dinners, comedy shows, and movies. It was because of a similar religious upbringing that we got along so well. I stayed at the church for about two years until I moved from Cincinnati to Columbus, where I still reside. Being a part of that church allowed me to develop and grow my spiritual health in a challenging and meaningful way. It broadened my eyes to see that traditional values vary from many organizations. Through visiting a few different churches over the years, I saw several different sets of church rules and expectations within the same doctrinal teaching. It wasn't until I became a part of this one that I understood they were no less committed to my previous home church's biblical beliefs and truths. I found out for myself that each organization had a few different traditional codes or more lenient rules to follow, which was okay. Even though some were different from what I was used to, members were still deeply rooted in their faith. The church in Cincinnati often extended its efforts to canvass the community to invite people to church. After all, they reached me. So I enjoyed being a part of a group of people who loved God and showed love throughout the community. I couldn't have continued to have faith in myself during my college coursework without nurturing my religious beliefs.

A lot of people think that they have to have money or to pay to gain knowledge. Sometimes that is true in some cases, and at times, the investment is worth it. The truth is, much of what we need to know is already in a book, audiobook on CD, or other listening materials available at your local library. I used the library all the time during my two years at Miami. Even if you can't find what you need at the library, some successful people are willing to share how they have gotten their success on other media platforms. I heard someone say one time, "you have to surround yourself with the kind of people you want to become." I've seen and heard so many advertisements of this skill or that one being offered in my area by this famous person or tv personality. They promise to tell you how to make money; all you have to do is reserve your seat. I went to one or two of those meetings before, and the "star" wasn't even there; I can't say that every event is like that. There was instead a hype person telling all kinds of testimonials about how to make money. By the end of the two-hour seminar, I still didn't know how to re-create the skill talked about during the presentation. I was promised that if I bought the CD series for the show price of something terribly low, I would be well on my way. Now, I'm certainly not claiming that every seminar would be this way. I am saying check into the credibility of advertisements like these. I later found a series of books at my local library that went into extensive detail, telling step-by-step how to achieve the same success that was about to be sold to me. Educate yourself for free!

I spent my second year of college going to class, working on school papers, working my part-time job, attending church, socializing a little, and reading as much fiction and non-fiction as I could handle. I made the dean's lists both semesters in my second year of college too. I was able to keep a job to help pay for my expenses, offsetting my combined college grants and loans, and also managed to have a little fun as well. I remember working at Elder-

Beerman department stores, mainly in the baby department. I would see so many tempting sales that I could take advantage of. On top of the sales price, I could use my employee discount for extra savings. Nobody told me not to accept the credit card offers that would start pouring in during college. As I checked out my purchase, a cashier asked me if I wanted to save an additional percent off by signing up for an Elder-Beerman credit card. So, Elder-Beerman was my first credit card during college, with Sears landing in second place.

I started with a whopping $500 credit limit, and as you can guess, I maxed that out in no time flat. Buying things from luggage (I still own the luggage to this day), clothes, shoes, kitchen appliances, to anything else that I'm sure now I didn't really need. I felt I couldn't pass up on my 15 percent discount from being an employee, on top of the sales prices, and I didn't have to pay anything upfront. It sounded too good to be true, so I signed right up for my credit cards. One of my finance course concepts explained all the different interest rates and how much they often cost a person long-term. It wasn't until after that class I had learned my lesson on the interest rates game. I would be paying those credit cards and fees for years to come. I figured out sometime during my sophomore year that credit cards weren't worth the tremendous inflation everything would cost me in the end. I didn't want to pay more than what the product was worth just to have it immediately. So I worked hard at putting most of the money I earned at work, not designated to bills, towards paying extra on these two cards. I eventually paid them both off and closed down both accounts.

I had plenty of friends those years that came over to our apartment to hang out and eat. I styled a few of the ladies' hair from our college campus for some extra cash too. I was so close to home that I probably visited once or twice per month initially, a little less often after I settled in my second year. I had my own car, a Ford Tempo that I drove from place to place until someone hit and totaled it. I was so proud of that car. My mother co-signed me since it was my first car purchase. I am glad she trusted me to make every single payment on time, which I did. That car and I had some great memories and good adventures together. The two years at Miami University in Middletown flew by with warped speed. Since it was a two-year college, I was fast approaching my Associate's degree in Business Management. I had visited the Miami main campus in Oxford quite a bit, making acquaintances that I'd fellowship with regularly. There were plenty of social activities happening there, especially on the weekends. As I was nearing graduation, I was a little saddened that my time here was coming to an end. I had made so many connections with people I enjoyed hanging out with. My best friend and I went to our graduation ceremony in 2001, and then after, we both had gotten our separate apartments near Cincinnati. I won't forget the education I got from Miami of Middletown because attending there put me on the path that would mold my future.

I would not have guessed that I wouldn't have kept in contact with a single person after graduation (2001) other than my best friend and one other I met while attending. Nobody told me that so many relationships would only last for a while. Some run their course in due time or after a stage in life like college. I've seen many people keep connected to the ones they went to college with, and mine was with my best friend after all these years. Sometimes people just seem to drift apart by distance, marriages, or even growth. Even the close relationships I enjoyed didn't last forever. I found myself trying to keep in contact with friends who didn't, for whatever reason, prioritize me into their lives as well. There have been times when I've tried to connect or have extended invites for lunch, coffee, or catching up, but life goes on, and it kind of tells me to move forward and keep memories for what they are - memories. I know life gets busy and everyone grows and evolves. One lesson I've learned along the way is that sometimes people are only in my life for a season or seasons. I found that it's not healthy to try and hold on to people that don't want to hold on to me. I truly believe people brush in and out of our lives, and the ones we need or need us plant roots, so we keep each other strong and help each other grow during our journeys. All of the many people who have been in my life have in one way or another been a blessing to me. I will certainly remember my college years at Miami, they were instrumental to the person I am now.

Chapter 6
Mr. Fine

After I received my Associates in Business Management, I was trying to figure out my next steps. I was employed at the Elizabeth Arden salons in Cincinnati, Ohio, and really liked the people I worked with. I knew it wouldn't be my forever job because I still had a long-term goal to be a business owner. Meanwhile, a friend of mine was receiving her Bachelors from Miami Oxford, Ohio. So along with two other close friends, I went to Oxford to cheer her on and congratulate her accomplishment. After the ceremony, my two friends and I all gathered outside next to her family members, who were jumping in and out of photos to take pictures of her in her cap and gown. The next thing I knew, I looked up to see this fine hunk of a chocolate manly man walk up next to her, looking handsome as ever. I was like, "wow! this guy is fine; he must be her boyfriend!" He was taking pictures with her, her family, and friends enjoying the mingling. When all the photo-snapping started to calm down, we were all invited to continue the celebration with her and her family at another location.

So, my two friends and I all headed back to the party to celebrate and eat cake. That's where I found out Mr. Fine was her younger brother. Everyone continued to talk and laugh. We were all having a good time and conversing, and Mr. Fine and I talked briefly with one another as people mingled around the room. I had mentioned to my friends that I needed to be back in Cincinnati to join my choir for the Sunday night service. So we said our farewells as the three of us headed out of the door. As I was walking to our vehicle with my two friends, the graduate came running to our car and asked if she could give my number to her brother. I responded by telling her if he wanted it, he had to come get it himself. She laughed, and went back inside.

Mr. Fine came out with this small talk, probably a little timid with my other two friends watching as we conversed. He finally asked for my number, which luckily for him, I gave, just kidding but not really. Then he proceeded to give me his cell, home, and a pager number too. I was asking myself why did he give me so many numbers? I'd guessed he was making sure I could get a hold of him. Afterward, my friends and I laughed and teased halfway back to Cincinnati. I was really glad I'd decided to go to Oxford, Ohio that day.

Over the next few weeks, Mr. Fine and I talked many hours over the phone almost daily. We were in the stage where conversations were easy, laughs were plenty, and at least I was both giddy and nervous every time I heard his voice. My stomach would jump a little with the excitement of be able to talk with him. We got to know each other's likes, dislikes, similarities, differences, etc. I know I got more than my money's worth from my cell phone usage during that time. I was on a cell phone plan that was only free mobile-to-mobile back then, and it worked well since we had the same carriers. Our conversations were going so well I set up a visit for him to visit Cincinnati a few weeks later. We hit it off quite well while I was showing him around the city and all it had to offer. We decided to make it official, and became an item. I hear many people use the word "smitten," that's how I would describe how I felt about this man.

Over the next few months, he continued to drive down to visit on the weekends. For me, the week seemed particularly long because all I could think about was that I would see him on the weekend. As long as those weekdays felt, I continued working hard and going about the routines I normally did, all the while trying to think of the city's best attributes I could show him to entice him to move to Cincinnati to close the distance between us.

The years following were like most romances. There was so much I liked about Mr. Fine. He always had me laughing with his jokes and light-heartedness. He was responsible for his finances and didn't mind picking up some of the tabs when we went out. Because I had been so independent, I insisted on picking some up as well. He showed me respect and affection all the time, and I could tell by the way he treated his mother that he would do the same to me.

Mr. Fine was working at a car dealership in Columbus at the time as a service advisor. I was still living and working in Cincinnati at the Elizabeth Arden beauty salons as a cosmetologist. I won't call the distance "long," but we traveled between the two cities for about a year or so after we began dating, with Mr. Fine doing most of the driving since I had my own place and he didn't. We went out to dinner, movies, shopping, concerts, and all the other normal things that couples do. After being unsuccessful in convincing him to move to my city, I finally moved to Columbus. I wanted to spend more time with him outside of weekends. So I figured, "why not?" I'm always up for something new; I was spending less time with my current friends and wasn't seriously committed to much of anything in the city aside from my church. Plus, I was still so close by, so I could visit my relatives and friends I had there in Cincinnati as frequently as I would like. I was all in for a new environment and had liked what I'd seen of Columbus so far.

I found an apartment on the north side of Columbus and settled in fairly quickly. It wasn't very big with its one bedroom, one bath, and a small balcony on the top floor unit. It was comfortable enough and affordable, so I signed the one-year lease and moved in. Mr. Fine still didn't have his place when I arrived in Columbus, so we spent most of our time at mine. I had already been on my own for a while, so I continued to enjoy cooking, cleaning, and laundry amongst every other house-keeping chore. It didn't take me long to obtain a job at Fiesta hair salons with my salon experience. I got to know Mr. Fine's habits, good and bad, and his pet peeves even better over the next couple of years. I met some of his family, and he met some of mine. Everything was going well between us, and I was pretty happy at my job. I had been visiting a few churches in the city but hadn't quite settled into one yet.

I was making quite a few new friends at the hair salons I worked. I ended up at SmartStyle family hair salons, starting as salon manager. I really enjoyed the experience of my job duties. I was tasked with making the 7-day schedule, ordering all the retail and back-bar products bi-weekly, and keeping the salon's inventory needs. As our relationship started getting more serious, we joined one another's families for holidays rotating from mine to his family gatherings. We'd vacationed together in Mexico, Chicago, and Indiana. We celebrated special occasions like me earning my associates degree and generally were together most of the time.

About four years in, we vacationed to Chicago again, where he proposed to me. We took other trips and vacationed in different places like Cozumel and Ensenada, Mexico, but Chicago held a special place in my heart because the engagement happened here. He later told me he'd tried to propose several times, and I kept messing it up. Once he tried getting me to go up to the top of the Sears Tower, I refused because I'd been up there our last visit, plus I'm not a fan of heights. He finally settled on dropping the ring in a glass that night after the other attempts failed. While I was enjoying a drink one night in our hotel room, Mr. Fine asked me did I see anything in my glass when I finally caught on to what he was doing. Of course, I said yes. I returned from vacation engaged, and the two of us couldn't be happier. I was four years into the longest relationship I ever had. Like any other couple, we had some disagreements that sometimes caused us to not speak for a day or two.

Those days felt like losing someone close when a day went by without conversation. I missed the connection we had if we didn't talk every day. No one tells you that those feelings of longing you feel can last if you choose to let them. Or that it's actually easy to forgive once you find out you too will require forgiveness at some point. I excitedly told my family and friends of my new engagement when I got back. My co-workers were so excited for me, as was my family. I signed the two of us up for marital counseling to explore relationship pitfalls I may not have been aware of. The counseling brought to light a few areas that we had different expectations on. Our counselor also gave us homework that had me thinking of scenarios I might not otherwise have considered. With our differences in-toe, we moved forward with our engagement plans.

Chapter 7
I Do

After we got engaged, Mr. Fine and I planned our wedding over the next year, saving and paying for our venue and honeymoon, managing to tie the knot in 2005 on a golf course. A lot of people spend thousands of dollars planning their wedding. We stuck to what we could pay for in full because we didn't want to still be paying for the wedding after we tied the knot. Both of our mothers insisted on helping, covering the costs as well. So extra hours were put in at work, and less miscellaneous spending happened over the next year to accomplish the goal. It was a beautiful ceremony taking place on a bright and sunny day in September. All of the white chairs lined either side of the aisle. Music was playing in the background as guests arrived. I walked down the aisle to one of my favorite songs, "I can't stop loving you" by KEM.

I made sure the program wasn't too long, even with the vows being said. Everything was perfect. I was standing on a golf course staring in the eye of the man with who I would spend the rest of my life. Our wedding day was beautiful. Perfect weather and location; maybe a hundred of our closest friends and family in attendance. Lily flowers, purple and silver colors draped everywhere. There was a beautiful and delicious purple and white wedding cake and soft music playing as guests arrived. I couldn't ask for anything more. My dress was perfect. I loved my shoes, loved my hair, and my makeup. Many whom I loved were surrounding me that day; we looked into each other's eyes, crying through our vows and promising that we'd love each other through the good times and the bad times.

Once the vows were said, our family and friends went indoors while the bridal party took several pictures outside. There was a buffet dinner waiting inside for us to celebrate. The dining room was decorated with my favorite color, purple, accented by silver, along with the all-white chairs. There was plenty of food, music, and fun for all to enjoy. After we had our first dance, garter, the bridal bouquet was thrown, and the ceremony finished, we headed home on a high note. A few of our family members drove our wedding gifts and leftover food back to our home. I was exhausted from the last few days and the time leading up to the ceremony wanting everything to be perfect. My husband wanted to watch an OSU football game, so I went straight to bed after our families left, falling asleep as soon as my head hit the pillow. The next morning, we were flying out to the Bahamas to enjoy our honeymoon. We spent about five days there enjoying the beach, food, culture, and relaxation. We had a blast and returned to start our lives as a married couple. The next few years, I worked, laughed, and smiled that endearing way new love shows, all the while enjoying our new union.

New life

About three years after Mr. Fine and I married, we found out that I was pregnant. I was happy, excited, and nervous at the same time. We hadn't planned nor prevented this pregnancy; nevertheless, we were both happy and excited about how our world was about to change. I had three years of marriage exclusivity getting to know my husband and knew a child would be an extension of us that we would be responsible for. My pregnancy went very well. I was one of the few who experienced no "morning sickness." I know a lot of mom readers will probably throw this book at this point. My co-workers could hardly believe how I barely showed at five months pregnant. As far as the eye could see, only my stomach protrusion was the only sign I was with child. I could eat fairly healthy, enjoy most meals as usual, and not veer far from my normal routines. I remember craving canned green beans some days and fresh tomatoes with salt on others throughout my first trimester. I didn't need ice cream, chocolate, burgers, fries, or anything of the such. All through the first trimester, red and green are what I wanted more than anything. As a matter of fact, I took organic prenatal vitamins, drank plenty of water, the whole nine yards following the doctors' orders.

I felt great throughout the entire pregnancy. I was able to continue working at my job in a factory all the way up until eight and a half months. I only had one instance when I was about seven months pregnant where I fainted at work. I was in quality control at the time. I was walking around the factory checking various things when a supervisor called an impromptu meeting. I wasn't very hot or anything, all I knew was one minute I was standing there listening the next my eyes opened with me on the floor. I had no idea what happened. One of my co-workers told me he caught me before I hit the floor. My supervisor insisted on wheeling me up to the front office on a golf cart like an emergency truck even though I said I could walk. Everyone was making a huge fuss over me because I passed out while I was pregnant. When I saw my doctor the following week, she told me I probably was standing in the same spot too long, and all my blood drew to my feet. I didn't even ask how common that was; besides, it didn't happen again. I'm sure that it scared my co-workers far more than me, as the baby and I were both fine.

My days were normal aside from a few kicks to the belly here and there. It seemed as soon as I laid down at night, the baby was alert, using my stomach as a kicking bag. My nights toward the end were pretty uncomfortable because I couldn't lay on my stomach. My belly was too big to sleep on and I couldn't lay on my side because the weight of it would pull and stretch my stomach so uncomfortably. I remember in month eight sitting straight up, throwing my feet over the side of the bed to the floor, and bursting out crying. It was because every time I laid on my side, my stomach would sink to the bed, making the pull from the other side so uncomfortable; I kept tossing and turning. I must've really been tired of being pregnant on top of being sleepy. None of the pillow tricks were helping me sleep more comfortably. My husband at the time tried ineffectively to console me. After my temper tantrum, I was finally able to go back to sleep after finding a decent position. Little did I know I would sleep differently (lighter) from then on because of our son's birth.

My husband and I checked into the hospital to get ready for our son's birth on October 1, 2009. I was a week overdue and so ready to unload this bun from my oven! I got a pretty decent room, I loved my OBGYN, and then they give me some ice chips. I don't know whose idea it was to give birthing mom's ice chips. The fact was, it seemed a little outlandish to me because I had rather had nothing than to be teased with ice. I was induced around 8 p.m. Let me tell you, "I labored" through all night into the wee hours of the morning. The contractions I experienced cannot be compared to anything I've ever felt. To say it felt like the worse cramps in my lower abdomen, back, pelvis, and uterus I've ever felt in my life is an understatement. As the contractions came and went closer and closer together throughout the night and morning, I was reconsidering a natural birth. The movies I've seen with women having babies did not prepare me for what I was experiencing. I thought I could do a natural birth, consequently, by 3 to 4 centimeters, I was definitely asking for the nurse to order an epidural for me. I got the epidural around 4 centimeters, and oh boy, I could finally catch a little sleep!

After getting a little rest, it was mid-morning when I saw my husband in a chair along the wall. My mother had been called and made it to the hospital just before I started pushing. His mother was present as well. An hour or two later, I felt my water break. It felt just like a balloon bursting below. I didn't know if I would feel it since I had the epidural, but I knew right away. So nurses were called, and they came in to check me, and it was time to start the pushing.

Apparently, I was pushing incorrectly at first because I was told to stop and was directed by the doctor on how to push correctly. I must've got it right the second time around because she'd say I was doing good. Now, I know some women push on and on for hours, but fortunately for me, I pushed for less than an hour, and boom, I saw my son's head. When I saw his head, I couldn't believe still that I was doing this. "One more push," said my doctor. I gave it all my might and pushed as he burst into the world weighing 8lbs, 11 oz., and 21 inches long, and just like that, my life changed forever. My mom, mother-in-law, and husband were all in the room with me. I was thrilled to have both grandmas present as a few other family members joined us over the next two days.

I don't know what you've been told, but birth isn't the most beautiful thing I've seen. I've heard both men and women say, "seeing your child born is the most beautiful thing." I tend to disagree; it's messy and invasive, not to mention all the pain. Nobody told me when the placenta pops out afterward that it would catch me off guard. I yelled, "Yuck." No one prepared me for how my body would react for the next few days. How I would not sleep, have all kinds of leaks, and I'd also be the one in diapers. And ladies, since nobody told me not to lie to the nurses when they asked, "are you pumping every two hours?" I did lie; I told them I was when I wasn't. Let me tell you, DO NOT LIE! Pumping was hurting when I tried, so I told them I was doing it when I wasn't. Apparently, I didn't buy the popular breast pump brand I heard everyone rave about. The nurses helped me latch my son onto my breast for feeding, but he always fell asleep. So he got a lot of bottles those first two days. The nurse would tickle his feet to try and wake him to eat a little more, but he was far too comfortable sleeping. I'd visit him in the nursery and try to get him to latch on. Or several times per day, the nurses would bring him to my room for a while, he just wanted to sleep. So I mostly just watched him in awe those two days, feeding him when I could get him to eat a little here and there. I could never forget those first few hours with our new baby; every detail of those days forever etched in my brain.

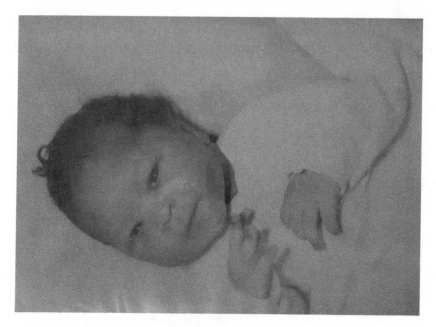

My baby picture

Hair stylist in the making

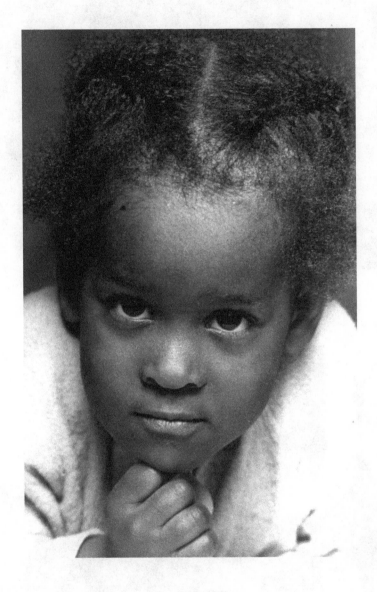

Me as a toddler

Dad and me, 12th birthday

High School graduation

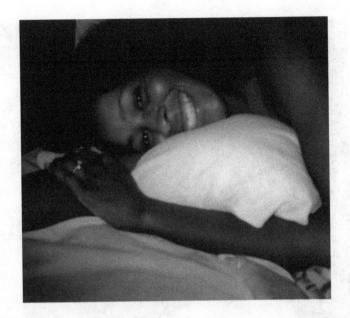

The night I got engaged

My wedding day

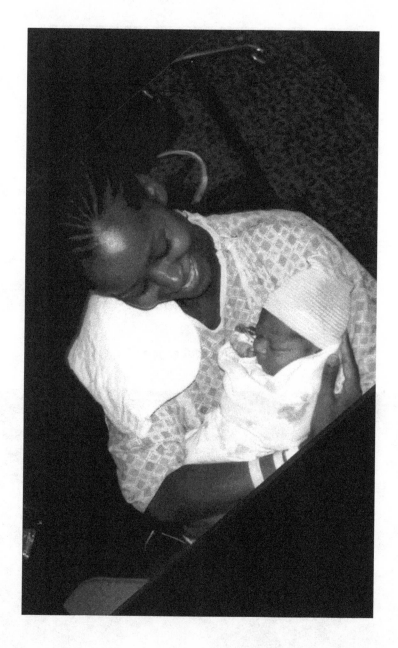

In hospital nursery

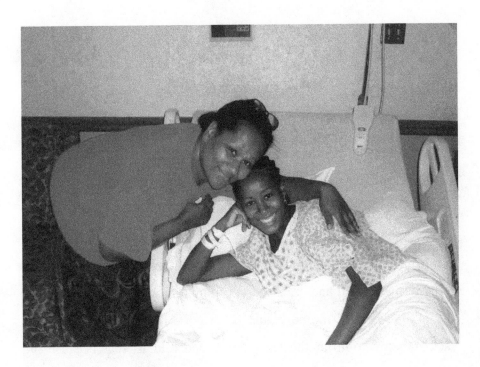

Mom & me after I birthed my son

Chapter 8
Bringing home a baby

As I was getting ready to be checked out of my room, the nurse told me our newborn son had to stay in the hospital another day or two because of his inability to keep enough milk down due to acid reflux. As a result, he wasn't gaining as much weight as they wanted him to. As you can imagine, I was all in tears about leaving him and going home. I cried and cried that morning and would not be consoled no matter who told me he would be in good hands. The nurse came back into my room at the last minute and told us that because our son's problem wasn't as serious as the other babies, and they needed the beds, he could go home. She said the nursery was crowded with premature and other babies who needed more specialized care from the hospital staff. I was whole again. I couldn't even imagine how any new mom would feel after leaving part of herself behind. I only got a glimpse of how that feels. As a result, I now respect moms everywhere that do this exactly to give their little one's all the support they need. Who so faithfully trust their doctors, nurses, and hospital staff to take care of their babies. Rightly so, they do a phenomenal job; I know because I had such a good experience.

I remember it like it was yesterday. We pulled gratefully into the cul-de-sac after three days in the hospital. I appreciated life's gifts so much more that morning. My wonderful neighbors were so excited for us when we pulled up in the driveway. I heard congratulations being yelled as you could imagine, with us bringing our first child home. We'd lived in a close-knit cul-de-sac for about four or five years. All of us neighbors talked in the front yards often, catching up with neighborhood happening. So the children on the block were excited to see our new bundle. Thank God for my wonderful sister-in-law warding off all the germ-filled kids from getting too close to our baby! She stopped them in their tracks to let them know it would be a few days before they could see him while thanking them for waiting. It's amazing how one little bundle can pull the heart strings of so many. There's literally not enough baby to pass around to all the hands that wanted to hold him. He was passed between my mother, sister-in-law, my husband, and myself as we settled in. If there were a staring contest, everyone in the room would win because new life is just that amazing. The family we had in the room was just gazing at our new baby. I enjoyed sharing every minute.

Here is why I said earlier don't lie to the nurses about pumping. When we got discharged, and I got home, I got engorged. Thank God my mom was with me! Moms who have breastfed know what I mean. Now I knew what my mother experienced all those years ago when I stopped cold turkey. All of a sudden, my breast were hurting so bad, they felt like rocks, literally. I was doubled over in pain while my mom was massaging and trying to get the milk down and applying hot towels. I'm sure I heard my husband somewhere in the background laughing and taking pictures, but I didn't care. Once we got some milk expressed, the pain lessoned. After that, I pumped every two hours religiously. Since I planned to go back to work in eight weeks, I only planned to breastfeed during the time I was home. That was a big mistake on my part because I found out formula is so expensive. Since nobody told me, I'd certainly recommend you continue to pump if you can. It's healthy, and it's free. It felt so weird to me buying my son's milk out of the center isles. I know there are a lot of great companies out there that develop awesome baby formulas. I'm certainly not knocking mothers who use formulas. I just felt guilty for not continuing to breastfeed because I loved organic and whole foods, and I had the most natural supply. My son has grown just as healthy with a mixture of breast milk and formula, just as many babies have before him. More importantly, if you want to breastfeed, invest in a good quality pump so that it's comfortable on your body. Invest in a good cooler bag to store your milk while at work or otherwise away from home. Don't worry; you can thank me later.

After the noise cleared, all the guest and family dispersed home; it was time for everyone to go to bed. Bringing our son home had been an exciting day. Of course, that night, dad slept like a baby. Not me, I had to listen to make sure I heard our baby breathing, see his body, oh so slightly, rising up and down, and ensure he doesn't tangle himself in the newborn blankets inside his bassinet. I consciously wanted to sleep because my body was so tired from the past three days. Nobody told me I would keep awaking every few minutes that I fell asleep just to check on our new baby. I didn't know then that I would still wake a couple of times per night to check on my son even to this day. (He's nine at the time I'm writing this book) It's ok if you sleep all through the night; believe me, get your rest! Some may call it overbearing or smothering, but something inside my maternal body changed permanently, linking me to our son's every breath. I'd wake when I'd hear him groan, shift, and cry to check that everything was okay. Even today, he often talks in his sleep, which also awakens me most nights.

The next few days after we brought our son home from the hospital were so worrisome. After almost every feeding, he was spitting a lot of the milk back up, keeping him from gaining the expected weight. Our son's acid reflux wasn't as serious as other babies; I was grateful he didn't seem to be hungry because of it. The nurse gave us directions to burp him every two ounces of milk he drank and make sure he sat upright after eating. They assured me that would help with his feeding and gaining weight. He continued to have a hard time with his feeding for a month or so after we got home. Aside from the feeding concerns, he was progressing well and I was so delighted to have him with me.

Our son made good progress, eventually gaining his proper weight and getting back on track with his growing schedule. I, on the other hand, was experiencing slight post-partum depression. I remember one night, in particular, my son was crying, and it was his dad's turn to console him. I asked him to take him out of our room so I didn't hear the crying, allowing me to get some sleep. I knew if I heard him cry, my brain would alert me to attention. Some sort of mother's instinct happened within my body that couldn't rest while he was crying. When he didn't take the baby out of the room as I requested, I just snapped. I started whaling on him, punching him all over with the baby in his hands. I was so mad that he was causing us both to lose sleep. I hadn't even considered that I could've possibly hit my son. Well, after my attack, he finally left the room and headed to the lower level, and I went back to sleep. How I slept after that incident, I'll never know. At the time, I hadn't even considered that I could have some form of post-partum, although looking back at that and another particularly embarrassing action on my part, it definitely was. I'm grateful that nobody was hurt aside from maybe a few feelings because of me; for any new moms who might be feeling a little off after having a baby, just check-in with your doctor and be patient with yourself and others. No one told me that it could be so embarrassing for such hormonal changes to occur and that I would have little to no control over them.

Our son was a happy baby; he ate, slept, cried, and smiled at his own leisure. You may think that crying would obviously wake a new mother; think again. I've seen first-hand how exhaustive it can be caring for my new baby, sleeping right through his cries. Let's not forget the seemingly never-ending diaper changes that kept me going back and forth to the changing table. I've been peed on, pooped on, and vomited on. So there is a lot that tired me out physically and mentally. When the body is tired, it's tired. I had certainly learned that bringing home a baby brings out many new thoughts and emotions that I couldn't have been less prepared for.

The three of us were together for the next six weeks; I was in awe of just watching him sleep, eat, smile, and any other movement he made. I returned to work after six weeks, mostly because I was afraid to stay home for the full eight weeks I could've taken. I was concerned that if someone else did my job as quality control for too long, I would no longer be needed. In reality, my job was protected because of the company's maternity leave practices. Even though I was a new mother, I felt antsy being home all day for so long and looked forward to going back to work. I felt so comfortable going back because I left my son daily with my husband to care for him. He'd gotten laid-off his job a few days after our son's birth which was unexpected. I continued to work full time during the day and take over my son's care when I got home from work each day. I knew our son was getting the best love and care, which allowed me to transition back into my job quite easily. Our son wasn't a great sleeper at night; he dosed in spurts of a few hours here and there. I thought he would get used to the sleeping routines I had in place by six or seven months. Aside from the daytime naps I tried to keep away from his bedtimes, he wasn't a heavy sleeper. He was growing up so fast, taking his first steps at eight months old. From there, he was walking all around the house exploring but somehow managed to understand when we told him not to touch dangerous things like the light sockets.

When my son was just shy of two years old, he was sitting in his high chair just off the kitchen counter by the dining room table, eating. He had his little snack on the table part of his high chair, and I was in the kitchen cooking dinner. I remember that day so vividly, not because I was making spaghetti, but because something happened that I will probably never forget. I had the hamburger browning in one pot and the water for the noodles boiling in another. I looked over every so often over at my son, just as happy as he could be. I dropped the noodles into the pot and let them cook the required time until they were ready to drain. Then I put the strainer into the sink, got my pot holder, reached to grab the hot pot to take it diagonally to the sink, which wasn't very far away. Somehow during the transition, I dropped the whole pot of boiling water, noodles, and all. My breath caught; everything went sliding across the counter, the hot water, hot noodles, everything was headed right towards my son's high chair. I couldn't breathe or move. I still had the hot pot in my hands, terrified about the hot mixture landing on my son because the counter sat higher than the chair. I just knew he was going to be burned, and it would be my fault. Suddenly, just before the edge of the counter, it stopped. I dropped the pot into the sink and immediately hunched over the counter, and started crying. I couldn't believe how close I'd become to scolding my son with hot water. I couldn't even continue dinner; I was so devastated. I called his dad from upstairs to the kitchen and told him what had just happened. He didn't understand why I was so upset; then again, he never did. There's nothing extraordinary about this almost very bad outcome of an event. What is extraordinary is that it could've turned out a lot worse. Not only that, my son was looking at me like I was having a crazy breakdown. After a while, I pulled myself together and vowed to be more careful when cooking around my son. I knew I couldn't always prevent him from getting hurt in ordinary accidents around the house; even so, it took extraordinary wisdom to accept I couldn't prevent them all, boy did I try.

When he turned one-year-old, we had a small gathering to celebrate at our home. He ate a little cake for the first time, and I took plenty of photos. He gave me no real push back to potty-training at two, and he got the just of things relatively quickly. I can only recall one or two falling out tantrums a time or two during the toddler stages.

At three, we decided that our son needed to be around other children to develop social habits better. Until then, he was mostly around adults of our families and their children, occasionally with some older cousins. When the day came to send him off to daycare, my son and both cried when it was time for me to depart. Of course, I waited until I got out of his view so he could feel more secure. I knew if he saw me crying, he would've thought something was wrong.

We both did a little better as the week progressed. By the time he started kindergarten, he knew that I would be back to pick him up. Although his first official day was emotional for us both, we at least held back the tears. He had already met his teacher beforehand. That morning of his first day, he looked a little unsure of how things would go, but he held himself together pretty well, and so did I. He's a pro at school now and loves going to see his friends. No one told me I would be so proud of my son and how he is growing and coming into his own personality. I didn't know it would be like this. That I'd be loving a person so infinitely wanting to make their life as joyous as possible. Wow! Love!

I decided to go back to school and finish my bachelor's degree after getting my son adjusted to daycare. Before I got pregnant, I had started that degree, so I put it aside to enjoy my pregnancy and time with our new child fully. It was not easy to take night classes, take care of my son, and work full-time, but once I'd put my mind to finishing, I could not slow down. I hadn't planned on attending my graduation ceremony when I finished my bachelor's degree at Franklin University. I had already had a celebration following my associate's degree a few years earlier at Miami Middletown and never intended to go back for a four-year degree.

My love for learning and eagerness to explore more business courses it what propelled me back into the classroom. I didn't want anyone making a huge fuss over me because some of my friends and family had already come out to celebrate with me for my first college degree. I didn't feel the need for a big to-do over every little accomplishment I made. However, I was proud of myself for returning while our son was still young. At the last minute, I was convinced to attend my ceremony by friends. A few friends and close family members gathered at the house afterward. I found it wasn't just about me as it allowed others who were proud of me to celebrate and congratulate me. The graduation ceremony seemed more for those attending to yell and scream in support when they heard my name called. I have to admit, I enjoyed the kind words and congratulatory hugs afterward, my quiet attention. Meanwhile, my marriage to my husband was feeling strained among our poor communication and disagreements piling up.

Outwardly, I seemed to have everything I could want, only at home there were days my husband and I barely spoke to one another, unless about our son. We had some disagreements before our son was born, but after, we had a lot more. I was spending a lot of my effort on my son, so my husband got the number two spot in a sense. I didn't see anything wrong with that since our son became my priority. He was so little, and I wanted to make sure I spent a significant amount of time with him, enjoying all his milestones. I seemed to be always frustrated after returning home from working a full-time job only to see my husband watching television or leaving the house as soon as I got both feet in the door. I knew he needed a break from our son; similarly, what about me? I was tired after work, only I still cooked and cleaned while balancing time with our son. The problem was, I expected to at least come home to a clean house, dinner cooked, family time with the three of us, and some appreciation. I started off encouraging him to get back to work; I guess I mentioned it so much after a while, it felt like I was pushing him to get a job, which I was. Even with all of his supposed free time, it was harder to spend quality time with my husband, with him not being around as much at the same time I was home. I'd often ask him if he wanted to attend a festival outdoors like the "Jazz & Rib Fest" or "Arts Festival" with our son and I, or other activities, only often he said no. I don't even remember what the "final straw" fight was about; I remember we stopped speaking to one another and started sleeping in separate rooms, and before long, it felt like we were nothing more than roommates. This went on for at least a year, after which I told him we needed to go our separate ways for a while to see what life was like. My heart sunk when he agreed without any reservations. I thought he would try to convince me not to go, at least because of our son, but I was wrong.

Nobody told me that marriage was one of the hardest job in the world, especially for women. I had to work a full-time job, cater to my husband's needs, do the laundry, clean the bathrooms, wash the dishes, cook dinner, whatever else needed to be done, and still have energy for a great sex life. These are just a few responsibilities that some may have. Don't get me wrong, I enjoyed doing all those things, but it was easy to feel unappreciated.

The wedding ceremony itself is beautiful, dreamy even. It's amazing looking around at all that you've planned for and seeing it turning out exactly how you'd imagined. It's lovely seeing everyone laughing and enjoying themselves. After the ceremony, I saw for myself; marriage is a serious commitment. I don't know that I was not really prepared for a feeling of not getting what I needed.

Like most new things, my marriage was shiny and new, and it started great. Our marriage stayed great for a long time too, as long as we agreed on everything and could work through the things we didn't. I've heard people say, "if you don't put time and effort into it, just like anything else, it will wither and die." No one told me I'd have to nurture my marriage just like I would a plant that is grown in my backyard. Once I plant a seed, I have to continue to water it, give it sunlight, and nurture it. I would need to fertilizer my relationship the same way I would my garden to build the confidence it needs to encourage growth. I would also have to remove the weeds or ignore the advice of some that have negative suggestions; speak in caring ways that showed I want nothing other than the best for my husband. I wanted to tell him lovingly when I thought he was wrong. Instead, at times it came out sounding critical.

Love is an action word. I'd have to show that I love by learning how to love my mate in the way that he needed, only I wasn't aware of that at the time. I could only see what I thought as love and how I wanted to express it to him. I had my thoughts on how love should look and be expressed to me too. Many people's version of love looks different from what their spouse see. In hindsight, I see we didn't communicate our needs to each other very well. At times, I felt my husband wanted me to be somebody I was not because I didn't feel accepted unconditionally.

Marriage isn't all about "being happy," rather it's about being self-less. Happiness is part of marriage; it only occurs from within. I didn't own that I and I alone was responsible for my happiness, which was something my spouse couldn't give me. I later learned that putting my spouse's well-being before mine was the key to a happy marriage. Learning and practicing putting yourself last and your mate first takes practice. When both put each other first, it's amazingly beautiful. This happens more easily when you keep God first. I learned that piece of advice from my Grandpa. He told me that is the design of how marriage should be. When you love someone unconditionally and go out of your way to ensure their very best, happiness comes back to you automatically. Your spouse will see you taking care of the things that are important to them. In return, they should go above and beyond for you because they see you taking care of them. It would've helped me to be unselfish and desire to see my mate happy and free being himself.

Now, how does one do this without losing themselves? This is something I had to figure out on my own much later; nobody told me. I believe self-care is what a person can do to keep from losing themselves. When I make time to feed my soul and body the good nutrients, it deserves I can then love and care for others in the way that I need to. When I make time to socialize with friends, I'm more relaxed when I get home. So, if that means scheduling an hour massage, reading an hour alone, listening to my favorite song, or whatever it may be that relaxes me and keeps me grounded, I do it. Hopefully, someone will identify with at least part of what I'm writing, if not all, to save yourself some discomfort from the emotional cycles we go through.

Now, remember I am no psychologist. I didn't go to school to listen to your problems and give you advice. Yet, I have a few life experiences that have shown me how to understand and process life's ups and downs. My processing isn't perfect, but it makes the uncomfortable parts more manageable. I learned through my own marriage that no one is exempt from pain, loss, or failure. Rather we are kind, caring, thoughtful, proud, or mean and hateful; the sun rises on the just as well as the unjust. These are just a few things that nobody told me.

I couldn't have seen how my actions affected my husband without him challenging me to look with his perspective. I didn't often agree with his views because they just didn't make sense to me. To understand how I treated my marriage, I had to look back from where I came from. I had to reflect on what I saw during my parents' marriage to understand myself more clearly. I realized much later that once I saw and understood how my parents interacted, I'd understand some of the habits instilled in me. I could make adjustments where needed to become a better version of myself. That didn't happen overnight, and I'm still a work in progress.

When I was twelve, my parents split, and it was very difficult for me being a daddy's girl. My four siblings and I stayed with our mom. I blamed her for their spilt for many years; even though, clearly I understood she was so unhappy even at twelve-years-old. Nobody told me how hard it would be when kids took sides during their parents' divorce. I saw the split as her unwillingness to cooperate and give my dad whatever it was he wanted. I felt like I was the only one who sided with my dad. We had a very special bond because I felt like his favorite because my dad and I had so much in common. Our love of jazz music, our thinking process, and our unwillingness to take answers without researching ourselves were only a few of the commonalities. When my parents split up, I felt he was taken from me without considering my feelings or how it would affect me. I never thought that seeing how my parents communicated ineffectively would affect how I communicated in my relationships.

Why is the obvious so blurred when you're amidst experiences? If only the obvious would make sense before the smoke cleared. I learned I was good at nurturing my home. There were times my husband didn't want or need me to care for him in the way I wanted to express. At times after our conversations, I felt like I was on Mars and he was on Venus. What do you do when after talking and explaining the best way you can, neither person is willing to see things from the other perspective? It's hard to empathize when I know I'm right or the other person knows they're right. So, where do you get perspective? In hindsight, I see that either both sides give in and develop a new solution, or one side succumbs to the other ideas.

During the time we were dating, I don't think I always revealed my whole self. I only revealed the parts of me I thought he wanted to see. I tucked some of the other parts of me away. I wouldn't call those other parts of me ugly, but they were definitely not lady-like. For example, whenever I got mad, I tended to throw things and sulk for a while. I probably hinted at these bad habits while we were dating. The habits apparently didn't scare him away. I was too busy impressing him and showing how wonderful I was. I can be loving, giving, humble, confident, or so many other attributes, but I can also be selfish, mean, and moody. Let me explain. I'd show my love by intimate affection, untwisting and emptying the pockets of his pants before loading them into the washer. I often cooked a meal that I knew he would love. I gave by working extra hours when I knew it would benefit us for vacations or other plans. I was humbled by not gloating in my accomplishments, such as going further in my education or being the bigger person by not saying "I told you so" when I was right. I was selfish in the fact of acting like a spoiled brat at times when I didn't get what I wanted. At the time, I couldn't see my tantrums were causing havoc on him; all I could see is that I was trying to prove my point. Often my reaction was giving the silent treatment after a disagreement. At other times I was plain mean by throwing things such as irons, cups of coffee, shoes, or anything else close by that wasn't bolted down during arguments. I learned a lot about myself during the 14 years we spent together. Most of which I didn't analyze until our marriage was at its end.

Heartbreak

About a year later, in 2016, I'm still married, only separated from my husband, we share custody of our son. He is amazing and an only child. Our son is such a beautiful soul. He is smart, has a sense of humor, and has always understood things I thought wouldn't occur to him until he was older. I tuck him in nightly, tell him how much I love him, kiss him on the forehead, and off I go to my nightly routines; alone. I ask myself often, "how did I get here?" We promised "forever" through life's good and bad, sickness or health, yet here I was ending my forever.

I thought that pre-marital counseling guaranteed that my marriage would last. I thought I was doing the "right" thing by having a minister at my church leading those pre-marital sessions. He was great; very knowledgeable about the topic of marriage as he was married himself for many years. No one told me that six weeks of counseling wouldn't be enough to hold my marriage together. I wasn't even sure if I wanted to hold it together myself at the end. The thing I knew for sure is that he wasn't willing to fight for me. So why should I fight for someone willing to let me leave so easily? I couldn't; I no longer had the energy. He wasn't willing to fight for our son's strong family foundation. There were so many questions that nobody told me I would ask myself. Should I stay for our son? I didn't know if staying for our son's sake would be the right thing to do because he was picking up on the two of us not hugging, kissing, or showing intimate affections. I didn't want our son to think that was what a commitment looked like. Will our son be okay? I also didn't want him to take any of his future commitments lightly because of ours ending.

Was I making the right decision? To be more transparent and truthful with myself and my son, I knew that I was. Why had it seemed so easy for him to see me leave? Was I not everything to him as he was to me? I don't know that I'll get the answers to those two questions, but it never made me question my self-worth. It took a few years to see that our son would be okay. It was a while before I saw that the best thing for our son was for me to be in a place where I could exhibit real love, happiness, and honesty.

The years ahead confirmed that I had made the right decision even though I had no closure. The weight of so much guilt was heavy for me to carry as I walked out the door. I carried that guilt for a few years until I was finally able to set it down. I know I was worth fighting for, and I would've stayed if he asked me to, but I wasn't about to fight for someone who didn't fight for me. Plus, in my heart, I knew he had left me long before I walked out those doors.

Chapter 9
Strong Roots

It's often said that it's hard to know where you're going if you don't know where you're from. I dedicate this chapter to my grandparents on my dad's side of the family. My dad's mom lived to be 94 years old. As I started this book, my Grandfather has neared two birthdays, fast approaching 97 years old, and is still living a full life. He attends church when he can, sometimes shovels the driveway in winter, and whatever else keeps him moving. Every time I call my grandad, a smile automatically appears on my face. I don't know a man of deeper faith and love for God and his family. He's shown and told me what Godly Love and relational love means and should be all the years of my life.

Of all the summers I spent with my grandparents, I can't remember one time he ever raised his voice, disputed, or was anything other than graceful to my grandmother. In fact, every time he looked at her, I saw the love he had for her. My grandad always credits God for the 70 years he and grandma spent married together. As a matter of fact, he credits God for all of his accomplishments.

My grandad was born to Mamie Lee Bailey and Augustus M. Williams. Most of his mom's side of the family migrated to Lexington, Kentucky, where my grandad was raised. My grandma was also born to Carrie Mae Davis and Richard Taylor, a few months earlier than my grandad.

Grandad grew up attending church with his mom and younger brother every Sunday. My grandma was raised alongside her three sisters and eight brothers in Lexington, Kentucky as well. Grandad told me he got so sick when he was a toddler and wasn't expected to live; he proved everyone wrong. Then he got what his family thought was pneumonia around age nine, being severely sick again as a child. Nevertheless, he grew up in the early 1900s when the outhouse was still outside, necessary accommodations were made inside for those nighttime movements, and you had to put ice in the fridge to keep the food chilled. My grandad and his brother had an adventurous childhood filled with playing in barns, swimming in the pond, and sitting listening to older folk's stories talking about the way things were.

Most of the people in my grandad's family worked on farms, fished and hunted, and worked on railroads. My grandad told me several stories of his brother and him growing up. I listened to one occasion as he told my cousins and I of a time when the two of them were children. They were running outside somewhere or another when his brother, with a candy stick in his mouth, tripped over something and fell. He was taken to the hospital by a coalman, where it was found that the candy stick was millimeters away from his brain. His brother survived the fall; apparently, it wasn't his time to go yet.

With many talents like painting, drawing, and singing, his brother went on later to serve in the U.S. Navy for thirty years. Had a daughter of his own who finished high school and became a RN in the US Navy. He was a master chief gunners mate, rare to non-existent for a black man to have in those days. He also was a master chief gunner instructor at Miami University of Ohio. He was in his late forties and happily married when he passed. I never got the pleasure of meeting him, but I'm sure I would've been just as fond of him too.

My grandparents met while attending high school in Kentucky on an occasion called "Sadie Hawkins Day." On this day, it was customary for the girls to chase the boys around the schoolyard. My grandmother caught my grandad that day; he says he let her catch him. He took her to the school dance after, and that was the beginning of their love story. Just as my grandad was nearing the end of high school, he was drafted into the US Navy, serving for about three years at Great Lakes Naval Repair base near Chicago, Illinois, then had his first assignment in Boston, Massachusetts. I'm sure there were many letters between the two of them over that course of time. At the end of the three years, the opportunity came for him to come back home, and he took it without hesitation. After he arrived back in Kentucky, he finished high school and enrolled into Kentucky State, completing two years there before transferring to Tennessee State to finish. Meanwhile, my grandma enrolled and finished at Meharry Medical College in Nashville, Tennessee, finishing at Fisk. It's easy to see why my Grandad transferred colleges, watching how amazing my Grandma was during my summers as a child.

I find it extraordinary that my grandparents lived through segregation, hard racism, and other atrocities and still managed to have a love for people. After all, grandma became a nurse, and grandad became a Science and Physical Education teacher. She was the first black nurse at Holsten Valley Community Hospital in Kingsport, Tennessee.

After they got married, they had five children, my dad being the oldest, with one younger brother, and three younger sisters. I've sat through several occasions where he has shared his experience of living through such a torrential time in history with my cousins and I. Even though I have learned about our histories, I still couldn't fathom having to live through it. I imagine some of the creeds he learned from respected philosophers, teachers, and friends helped him thrive during those times. One of grandad's Jr. high teachers taught him, "do all the good you can to all the people you can, in all the ways you can just as long as you can." He remembered another creed throughout life "live most and serve best," by a great physical educator and life philosopher he was good friends with. No one told me I would have the pleasure of being a part of such a beautiful legacy and family forged by God and the union of my two grandparents some seventy years ago.

My grandparents supported their children, with my grandma working as a nurse at night and my grandad teaching in various teaching positions. He spent his longest stint at Lincoln Heights school and the Princeton school district for 23 years. They settled in Cincinnati, Ohio, in 1967, where they made Lincoln Heights Missionary Baptist church their place of worship. Grandad served as a Sunday school teacher, Trustee, Deacon and managed to sing in the male choir as well. Grandma served on the Nurses guild and did some public speaking throughout her career to recruit other women into nursing. Grandad managed to show his family love by taking his children fishing and giving them hugs. Of course, I, along with other grand and great-grands, still enjoy those hugs today.

Just as he was retiring, his pastor asked him to start a scouting program that became the Boy Scouts troop 772 chartered organization through his church at sixty-five years old. He remains representative with the boy scouts today, thirty years later and counting. During those thirty-plus years, over thirty boys have earned their eagle scout rank. He couldn't have accomplished all he had without God, my grandma by his side, as well as wonderful scout leaders in his troop for all those years. (committee chair, scoutmasters, advancement chairman, cub master, & DC) It's easy to see how the creeds and lessons he was taught have carried him now and still. Those creeds have also trickled down to his children, grandchildren, great grandchildren, and many others.

It's because of all the times that our family had gathered over the years together for weddings, graduations, anniversary celebrations of my grandparents, and funerals prompted all of the grandchildren to decide to plan a trip of our own. We've had so much fun sitting around laughing, talking, and catching up with each other until one day just wasn't enough. It was because of so much reflecting on all the love our families have shared, in 2019, all the cousins on my dad's side met in Gatlinburg, Tennessee, for our first annual cousins' reunion. It was the first time we met and stayed together for three nights in a large and spacious cabin. There were 38 of us in the three-story cabin. It was an extraordinary time for me to experience so many family members with different personalities, expectations and still meshing so well together. There seemed to be no preconceived notions other than to enjoy each other's company and catch up on things happening in one another's lives. It was awe-inspiring that I knew that every one of us stemmed from our grandparent's union. There was so much socializing going on around me; I sat at times just soaking it all in. The laughter and conversations, card game going strong, and so much teasing. There was so much love and support in the air; it was humbling to me: the legacy that started between my grandmother and grandfather falling in love and getting married. Each one of us in that cabin were raised with values, integrity, love, and so much more. I looked around at the teachers, professors, business owners, pilots, hard-working, and entrepreneurs in the room; it made me feel full. Nobody told me how my heart would feel so full of the love that family could bring. My grandparents didn't only teach us but showed all of my cousins and I how to be dedicated to our own families, giving to our children and communities, use our talents, and so much more. I could go on and on about how extraordinary our family is and is challenging their children to be as well. God has really blessed our family.

Chapter 10
Mother Dearest

My mom was born in the 1950s in Middletown, Ohio, to Robert E. Storey (1933) and Hortense Carter (1938). She was the oldest of three sisters in a house full of women. I can't even imagine how the world in the thirties shaped her parents' raising and guiding her on the path she traveled. My mother lived with her mom, who was strict about raising her. She had to come straight home from school every day so that her mom always knew where she was. Those were the rules for her even throughout high school unless she volunteered at the hospital as a candy striper. Her mom felt that she was safer coming straight home daily with no spontaneous stops. My mom tells me there were a lot of extended families involved in looking out for her and her sisters growing up, such as her "big mamma" (her mom's mother) and some aunts and uncles. Now I see why my mother was pretty strict with me because people often exhibit some of the same habits and practices they see growing up. I suppose I had a little more freedom than she did because I often stopped into the corner store on the way home from school to get snacks and things. One of the other freedoms my mother let me have was the traveling I did with my youth department at our church. We had several out-of-state overnight trips I could participate in over my teenage years because I had the money to go I earned from my jobs.

Just before I turned twelve, I was in our kitchen baking chocolate chip cookies from a box my mom just bought from Aldi. I only needed to add one egg and butter to the mixture before putting them into the oven. They must've smelled really good because my dad asked about them. I took a few upstairs to his work area and let him try a few. He said that the only thing that would make them better was some walnuts. Once I returned downstairs to the kitchen and told my mom what he said. She replied by telling me, "you should bake him a dozen just the way he likes them and charge him for them." Well, that was one of the things my mom said to me to spark my business interests.

The following week I went to Aldi with her, and we picked up a box of cookies and a bag of walnuts. As soon as we were home and I'd finished helping put the groceries away, I got right to work. I baked a dozen chocolate chip cookies with walnuts, marched right upstairs to my dad's work room, and told him he could buy them for a small fee. That was the beginning of my sales experience that day. My dad nickeled and dimed me until we agreed on a price. I later gradually increased the price slowly over time, making a little more money once I had him hooked. I baked him cookies almost every time we went to the store and made myself a little bit of pocket change. This was the beginning of my love to earn my own money. I'm forever grateful to her not only because of that but always doing her best to explain how to make more with what I had. I never saw my mom worrying if she couldn't pay a bill on time growing up.

Sometimes they just had to be paid late, yet I never saw her sulk and whine; she just worked on ways to get them paid.

Some of the ways that my mom guided me growing up were perhaps a little unconventional at times. All of the arguing I did with my mom growing up was the constant struggle of myself within raging to have a voice, an opinion that mattered. My words were not always kind, but my actions always spoke louder than my words. All of the going to church, enforcing rules at home, and disciplining me evaluated how I would set boundaries and guidelines for my own future family. Some of the very decisions she made I would carry into my habits of raising my son. One particular time, before my teens, my mom woke me up after I had gone to bed one night and told me to get downstairs and finish washing the silverware I'd left in the sink. It was my chore that week and I had washed all of the dishes except for the part I hated most, the silverware. To me, that was the grosses part of any eating ware I could touch because my whole family had them in their mouths. That wasn't the first time I'd left the silverware, so I supposed mom was disciplining me and teaching a lesson by waking me up.

A few years before that, I was the last of my siblings sitting at the dinner table because I didn't finish my peas. I absolutely hated those squishy canned peas. I sat there as my mom required, for what seemed like at least an hour or two. It's not that I was stubborn; I just couldn't stand the squishy soft texture nor the taste of canned peas. I don't know if my mom was stubborn, relentless, or just didn't want me to waste food. I'd eventually, after some time sitting there, stuffed all of the peas into my mouth, put my plate into the sink, then go right to the bathroom and flushed them down the toilet.

If there was some sort of lesson to be learned in that, I think I missed it. I felt I had so many character traits from my dad that it was difficult for my mom and I to get along. I always believed the mannerisms and thought process I had reminded her of my dad when we conversed. All of the differences my mother and I had would continue throughout my teens; even so, there was one particular time all was well, Christmas.

Christmas mornings

Christmas morning growing up in our house was so much fun because my mom made it feel so special. I believe my mom slept downstairs on Christmas Eve, so we wouldn't sneak downstairs to shake the packages and guess at our gifts. We couldn't come downstairs Christmas morning until everyone was awake. I was the laid-back one out of all my brothers and sisters; being awoken by them, I was pushed out of bed. It wasn't that I didn't look forward to the ripping apart of all the gifts. I just enjoyed watching everyone else opening up their gifts and seeing the delighted looks of surprise on their faces more. My mom hung stockings with small items inside them, put up a full-size tree, and the room was so full of gifts, large and small.

She always made our Christmases so memorable. They seemed like the biggest day of the year to me, with all of the many gifts sprawled all around the tree. Mom always made Christmas holidays feel bigger than life and so extra special. That had a lasting impact on me.

I still don't know how she did it because I knew growing up, our family had not been as financially stable as some of my other friends. Nevertheless, I couldn't tell by the way my mother went all out at Christmas. I remember getting black dolls, cabbage patch kids, pajamas, an easy bake oven, and many other gifts that my mom put thought into. I know she knew me well and gave great thought because the gifts were things I'd like. I'd been into beauty and hair for as long as I can remember. I suppose I need to thank my mom, whom I must've got the hair gene from because she took cosmetology courses in high school the same as I did. It must've been obvious that I had a natural talent for hair and nails because one Christmas when I was about eleven years old, my mother got me a nail dryer and an electric nail shaping kit. I could put all four fingers and my thumb into dry after I polished my nails. The electric nail kit allowed me to file nails with an emery board, buff them, and shape them with several different tools. If anyone told me that my mother would invest in my talents, creativity, and dreams so lovingly early in my life, I probably would have thanked her so much more throughout my life.

My siblings and I played with our new toys and gifts all morning. There was usually snow outside on the ground and lots of it. So it was inevitable that we would dress in our snowsuits and play in the snow. Winter in Ohio today may or may not produce snow nowadays. When I was a kid, I enjoyed building snowmen and having snowball fights with my siblings and neighbors, especially on

Christmas. By the time our mom called us in, probably no more than thirty to forty-five minutes later so we didn't freeze to death, we'd be covered in snow from head to toe, noses running, and cold. Coming inside, pulling off our snow-covered boots, icy socks, and gloves was just as exciting. Our toes and fingers would be tingling while all of us ran for the heating registers on the floor to get that warm heat coming from the furnace. Sometimes I would grab a blanket or pull my pajama gown over my knees to cover the entire heating register so my whole body would feel the warm air. It felt heavenly.

Nobody told me that Christmas in my childhood would be so important and memorable to me. Now that I'm an adult, I appreciate my family's closeness because of my mother laying the framework. When my siblings and I became adults, and some of us had children of our own, we've continued some of my mom's traditions as well as starting a few of our own. It gets harder and harder to connect the whole family on Christmas day or any other holiday, for that matter. Nowadays, there are calls on Facebook Messenger, Skype, or the other services available to talk and see your loved one when you can't be near one another. It makes the Christmas holiday so much more special because I'm thinking of my loved ones both near and far.

Giving must've been the theme in my mother's household growing up because it was obvious to me at every holiday, birthday, or special occasion that mom had the heart to give. From a very young age, my mom taught me the lesson of "tithing." She trained me to set aside 10 percent of all my earnings right as they came into my hands. That way I wouldn't miss such a small amount if I already planned on giving it away. She explained that it didn't belong to me anyway by showing me a bible passage. I hear so many different philosophies on "tithing" or "giving." Some people do it, and some people don't.

Some are taught that when you give, it comes back to you. Some believe what's theirs belongs to them to do what as they please. From my experience of seeing my mother tithe and tithing myself, it didn't seem stressful or inconvenient. I always felt good when I gave that 10 percent away, believing it was going towards something useful. I cannot say that we've never been without what we needed because we have. However, I can say that we have always been blessed. I don't think that I've ever missed the 10 percent. When I think about it now, there isn't much I can do with ten percent of anything I have; besides saving or hoarding it. It's just not that significant to me. So why not continue giving in some form and believe that it will come back to me? No one tells you that sometimes giving money, time, or talent is a leap of blind faith into what we cannot see. You don't always see the end result of the giving, but you hope it's making a difference. Hoping that wherever the blessing is sent, it just lands into the hearts or hands of someone who benefits from what was sacrificed. Who knows how an amount as little as ten percent may cause growth or prosperity, fill a need, or even work together with someone else's gift to provide for someone or something in a huge way. I owe that thinking to my mother too for teaching me the art of giving.

My mother had a somewhat quiet demeanor raising me and somewhat still does to this day. Whenever I pushed the wrong buttons, I saw another side of her come out that was ferocious. Quiet certainly didn't mean she was a pushover; believe me, she wasn't. My mom didn't play around when it came to us behaving and carrying ourselves in a positive light. My mom taught me to be respectful to her and all adults. Even though I came from the generation of "because I said so," there was a lot in that lesson as well. When I asked my mom a question, and there was an answer I didn't like, she told me that she was in control of what I did and did not do. That was a really hard lesson for some to learn because naturally, I wanted answers and explanations.

At times I had to accept directions she or an authority figure gave. At times it's fit to challenge beliefs, and at times it isn't. If someone would've told me that I would appreciate some of the limitations that my mom gave me, I would've laughed, but truly I do, and there were a lot. The limitations taught me that I'd have to do some things you don't want to do sometimes in life because they just need to be done. She didn't allow me to do things, like cut my hair or pierce my ears, while teaching me to accept her authority. I appreciate all these small lessons from my mother. Some didn't have to be taught; I learned some just by watching her. More than once, I watched her secure a home for my four siblings and I.

When one door closed, she managed to find her way to another open one. She was resourceful like that. Even now that I'm an adult and have been out from under her roof for quite some time, I'm still learning from her. She gives me wisdom when I ask for advice in raising my son, tries to tell me to relax sometimes when I'm working hard, and insists that I be proud of my small successes. There were times in my youth where we didn't see eye to eye, and I pretty much questioned every direction she gave me. Looking back, I wish I hadn't given her so much grief. Yet, it was my way of expressing how my journey ahead would look a little different from the one she wanted for me in my own little way.

I'll never forget the time in my teens when mom slapped me in my mouth for talking back to her in front of other people. There a lesson there, too; I learned quickly never to do that again unless I wanted a repeat of being sorely embarrassed. In that way, learning my lessons only took me once because I never wanted an encore. Even now, I try to respect her more as an adult and have my child. I see firsthand how hard it is to balance being approachable and setting boundaries for my son.

At times I find that I give my son a few more freedoms than I had in hopes that he's more versed in the choices that will shape his life. On other occasions, I find myself using some of the same rules she laid for me with my son. As such an amazing woman who stands firm in her beliefs, I see my mother, forgives me countlessly, loves her children and family more than life, gives from her heart, and feels all life's little joys. I'm so proud to call her mother.

Chapter 11
Daddy's girl

My dad grew up during the Civil Rights Movements. He was learning and growing during the Jimmy Hendrix, Vietnam war, pot-smoking, and enjoying the new-found freedom era. He barely escaped involvement in the Vietnam War, instead enlisting in the Air force. He was already a well-versed young adult from moving around a few times in his childhood. My dad saw first-hand the women's voting rights come to life, and black and white people now being able to mingle with lessoned fear of the black man being killed.

He told me of the "Black Panther Party" and "Power to the people" movement, only I still can't imagine what that must've felt like first-hand. Being stationed south of Japan in his early twenties in the Air Force gave him experience with diverse people and cultures not easily forgotten.

When I was little, my father wore many hats. The earliest job I remember him having was driving the bus for the city of Dayton at RTA. His work never stopped there. It seemed no sooner he came in the door from work than he started working on his true love, typesetting, printing, and photography. There were a lot of days and nights I'd sneak down right outside his photography area and watch him taking pictures of people in his studio. Dad always had some instrumental music playing in the background, mostly jazz sounds, including the guitar or instrumental. He had a love for that kind of music, as did I.

My dad would play his guitar for us sometimes when he didn't have people in his photography studio. It would accompany the music playing on his stereo or just him playing solo, but mostly with music in the background. When he was in the studio, I'd hear him telling them to move this way or that way, or he'd be adjusting the lighting or camera lenses. I would see him moving a person's hair out of their face or physically moving their body to get just the right angle he wanted.

One day I was peeking in, and he was photographing Dorian Harewood. I didn't even know who he was back then, only to find out later he was an actor. Mr. Harewood and my mom were photographed together that year. Watching my dad moving around his studio in different capacities proved he was in his element. The way he conducted business had been etched in my brain, gearing towards my business interest for the future.

When I was little, my dad was the sparkle in my eyes; he seemed so amazing to me. I don't know what it was that kept me wanting to make him happy with me. I had to be around the age of eight; I thought I heard my dad say, "go and get the TV." So that's what I did without even second-guessing myself. After coming down the stairs rounding a corner to the living room, seeing both my parents all but have a stroke. He said, "I told you to get the TV guide, not the TV." I don't know what made me think that my little bitty self could carry the television all the way down the stairs, let alone think that he would ask me to. It was only a 10 or 12-inch black & white, but I wanted to do as I thought he asked. I don't think I realized how capable I was of carrying such a heavy load until I made it down the stairs without dropping it. Today, I don't ever think that there are any tasks impossible to accomplish. I guess I took that approach early on in life.

My dad always had at least two or three computers in his office, along with printers and other technology we weren't allowed to touch. There only were a few exceptions when he'd get his black joystick out with the red button, and he'd let us play some computer games for a few minutes. He'd stay in his office for hours on his days off as well as the days he went into work too. It seemed to me as a child; he only came out of his workspace to grab some food or use the restroom. There were occasions he'd come out to wrestle with my brothers, play rock paper scissors with us girls, and tickle or make us laugh before retreating back into his work. I felt much closer to him than I did to my mom for several years, even though she was home every day. I never blamed him for working because I understood he had to work to provide for our family. Plus, I could see how passionate he was about his businesses.

My dad's busy schedule kept him busy, but he always made the time he spent with us feel significant to me. I never knew if he put the money he made into the household or back into his business. I certainly didn't see or understand everything as a child, so I wouldn't know. I always assumed his business gave him so much joy and fulfillment being in his element at this project and that one. At that time, I was fascinated by his passion for his work, music, and world views. I paid attention to every detail to the words he spoke, the conviction of his ideas and thoughts; maybe that's why we seemed in-sync.

During hot summer days or Saturdays, my dad would take us on outings to see the city. He took us to parks to run around and play, airports to watch planes take off, Sonic to share burgers and fries, and so many other places that were usually free or low cost. I still had so much fun because it was like I had my own personal tour guide. He made it fun for me by giving a historical or fun fact about the places we would visit around the city. He'd light up with excitement when he told us the histories behind the planes or landmarks he took us to. Most of those times, we rode the city bus. I think it was free or nearly free for us to ride since he worked for RTA. My dad always said with so much pride when we got on the city buses, "these are my children," to his co-workers driving. Other times we packed into our brown Nova car for an outing. I knew my dad loved us; he told me the five of us were sweet-spirited children. I know that my dad did the best that he could with us. Those outings made me enjoy history as well as learning new things. I can credit my dad for feeding that part of me that never tires of learning.

I don't know why I had such a way with my dad, but even then, at less than twelve years old, I knew I could talk him into things my mom could not. A few times, my mom asked my dad for grocery money, only for him to give her a pitiful amount for a family of seven. I'd march right up to my dad's workroom and tell him we needed more money for groceries. I don't remember what I said, but I'd returned downstairs with my mother's amazement with more money when she couldn't. I must've been about the same age when my dad walked in on my mom, giving me a whipping. She must've been tearing me up because my dad made her stop. That's one reason why I viewed him as my protector because he stopped my mom from getting me, even if I deserved it.

My dad always had long family conversations with us on why he objected to religious traditions and many other topics. I seemed to understand at a young age why he didn't take rules, laws, and traditions for face value. I, too, questioned why a person would accept a certain church rule simply because the pastor said so, especially when the rule didn't come from the Bible. The debates were always much bigger than that, but my dad always questioned the status quo. I rarely remember my mom responding or even looking at him after a while. She looked so fed up of him constantly trying to prove his point. In that way, I sometimes guess as much as two people love each other, they just don't know how to love in the way the other person needs. I would sometimes hear my parent's arguments, and my dad would speak with such conviction to compel me to listen. He wasn't even talking to me, but the way he communicated made me want to listen and consider his views. He would try to get his point across; only the depth of his voice couldn't convey the level of conviction he had about what he believed. Sometimes he would lecture every one of us at home for hours. Some of my siblings would be falling asleep while our mother would be trying to cultivate an ending, never to her avail, because he would literally talk for hours. Some days, he insisted that we wait until he was finished; other days, we went to bed while my mother did the listening. At the time, I thought I understood dad's points and couldn't see why she didn't too. I would imagine he has several books in his brain crawling at each other to get out.

Nevertheless, the love I had and still have for my dad makes me appreciate all the passion he instilled in me. I could go on and on about something I'm passionate about with the right people to converse with. It could be possible that my dad and I had a closer relationship than all my other siblings because I was the one who listened to him so intently. I suppose that's where our connection cemented during those long hours that I was willing to listen and show interest in his topics. The way he talked and I listened with my eyes always paying attention, not missing a word. I now understand my mom wasn't a left thinker or didn't question rules or traditions because she just accepted the things that didn't feel wrong. She was used to following rules and not questioning them by the way her mother raised her.

My earliest memory of loss was when my dad and mom were separating, which meant my dad was moving out of the house. To this day, I can remember quite vividly when he left. He came into my bedroom to say bye as I was laying at the bottom of the bunk bed my sister and I shared. I had a horrible headache that day. My dad came in to say bye for now and kissed my forehead as tears rolled down my face, probably for both the pain of the headache and the loss of my father leaving. That was the last time I saw my dad regularly. After that day, I only saw him sparingly here or there over the years, or sometimes several went by, compared to before I saw and interacted with him nearly daily.

When two parents separate for whatever reason or reasons, it cheats children out of the time they have with one of their parents. Inevitably, one person gets custody limiting the other parent's parental rights. I'm not sure if my mom thought about how our father not being in the house would affect our social and emotional well-being. I am sure my father didn't want to leave as he told me that day and many years later. I don't know many situations where the children's time is equally divided between two parents. I never knew until I became an adult that dividing the time would be so hard.

From my own experience of ending my marriage, I know I considered my son very heavily in the decision I made. I decided to leave from such a calm and sure place in my heart and mind. To be the best mother I could for my son, I had to love and put myself first. No one told me that I would blame my mother for several years as a teen after seeing my dad leave and go away from me after their divorce during my teenage years. I didn't see him the same way that she saw him. Even though the two of them had their differences, I only had the perspective from a child's level. He was my protector, and I understood his views.

In a matter of days from my parents last argument, dad was gone. I hope that my son will realize throughout his life that I made the best decision I knew how, just as my mother did. I had to ensure my son had both of his parents involved in his everyday life more than mine. I missed over the next few years having the one person who understood me the most around. I missed hearing his jazz playing throughout the house or moments of sitting with him listening to him playing the guitar. It was a whole different dynamic around the house once my parents split. I knew my dad wasn't perfect, but who is? I had a hard time navigating mom's new rules, especially since she would only play Gospel music and not let me listen to anything aside from it either. I loved Gospel music but wanted to experience other music as well. I lost all those moments when dad came out of his workroom to tickle and play with me, moments of baking him chocolate chip cookies and just getting a glimpse of him every day. These and other memories had to be enough to see me through my journey since I wasn't given a choice any longer to be "daddy's girl."

Chapter 12

Dreams really do come true

I wonder, sometimes, does everyone dream? Will dreams come true if we have the courage and strength to pursue them? I am a dreamer. I have dreamed of owning my salon since I was in my teens. I dream of making the world a better place because of something I've contributed. I've dreamed of businesses. I've dreamed of owning real estate. I've dreamed of what I think my future should look like. I have found out firsthand that sometimes the things I chase are side-barred for a while so that something more intentional carves a path to my dream. If I had not been willing to veer off my chosen plans that I had, I may not have experienced these stepping stones that would get me to the place I've wanted to end up. Every day I feel like I'm closer to where I'm supposed to be. Sometimes my life guides me in different directions I never thought I'd travel, those directions adding a much needed pausing or resting point.

I think it's extraordinary that we all have some talent or gift inside us just waiting to be shared with the world. It is up to us to help make the world a better place, and we can do that in so many ways. I'm choosing to share what I think will help someone, even if it's just a few people. I'm hoping to encourage someone that they're not alone in life's journey's short or long. Small victories count in a major way, no matter how insignificant those victories feel. Everyone is uniquely and wonderfully made, so that means we are all extraordinary. There isn't a single person on earth who is just like me. My DNA is so unique that no one else is exactly like me.

After I got married, I was still looking for opportunities to fulfill my salon dreams. I happily worked in a beauty salon when an opportunity fell into my lap that I didn't even know I was passionate about. It ultimately gave me the financial freedom to be able to pursue my salon dreams. It was about 2006 when I first saw this television show on HGTV called "Flip that house." The show's basis was business partners who went out and searched for the ugliest house in the worst condition that no one else wanted, purchase and rehab it to sell and make a profit. I could watch episode after episode and be thrilled and excited each time I saw the before and after of one project after another. I was hooked on the show from the very first episode I watched. It was so crazy to me that the buyers would spend, for example, $100,000 on purchasing a house, spend $75,000 on fixing it up, and then selling it for $275,000. Most timelines were in as little as eight-weeks for completion on all needed renovations. I was so amazed. I thought to myself; I could do that. So, I looked to my then-husband, who was watching most of the episodes with me, and said, "we can do that." We looked around at our plain blocked and unfinished basement and decided to finish it.

The first thing we did was apply dry-lock to the block walls then put up beams along the walls. It was quite an exciting experience watching him make all the cuts as I helped hold the wooden 2x4's into place while he used a nail gun to secure them to the concrete floor. After we got the wooden beams secured, he started installing the electrical outlets along the beams, with me nervously assisting him. We also hung the drywall, started puttying and sanding all the joints. We installed a drop ceiling so that every wire or plumbing pipe under it could be accessed easily. Next, we laid carpet on the living side and vinyl sticky tile to the floors' laundry side. By the time we finished painting the basement walls, we had a pretty good finished product we were both proud of. All the while, we were saving money by doing the labor ourselves. That was the beginning of our house rehab mini addiction.

The first property we purchased together in 2007 when the housing market was on a major downturn only cost about $15,000. It was a two-story 3-bedroom home with a full basement and two-car garage. Although in an up-and-coming neighborhood, the price was unbelievable. It took about eight months to finish the first rehab from start to finish. We did a pretty good job for first-time rehabbers with no real experience other than our own home remodel. Once we got a tenant into that first property, we kept her for eight years. After that first experience, we got better and better at the finishing processes like painting, floor molding, lawn care, and refinishing surfaces. I loved seeing old wooden floors being brought back to life by my sanding and staining hard work. It seemed amazing how fifty or one-hundred-year-old wood could be so worn, scratched, abandoned, and dinged only to be brought back to life so brilliantly. That was perhaps one of my favorite parts of rehabbing because I love old wood. Also, we got better at choosing contractors for major repair work.

Over the next few years, we purchased, rehabbed, and rented several properties together, not paying more than $22,000, which was still far below market value. I was hooked on seeking and finding properties that we could bring back to life. I don't know if the market will ever be like that again. At the same time, we were making additional income by preparing living quarters for someone to live and call theirs, we were expanding our knowledge about the process. After we got a good procedure in place, the properties were completed more efficiently and became available much quicker.

There is a lot involved in purchasing and rehabbing a property that you don't live in. Not everyone is cut out for managing more than one home. I had to be diligent in checking in on each property every day when one was in rehab mode. I had to check on contractor's work, be ensured they complied with city permits, be knowledgeable about the work that needed to be done and the average costs.

In addition to everything else, I prepared for overages and so many other things that came up. Our second property had a busted sewer line in the pipes out in the front yard, almost to the sidewalk. We thought the city would be responsible for the cost, but it turned out we were responsible for the $2,000 overage. Turned out the city only covered lines under the sidewalk out to the street, so we had to pay for the ones under our lawn. A lot was learned throughout the first few flips. I was in no way an expert even after finishing eight properties, although what I did was completed very well. Each time a lease was signed with a new tenant, I felt more and more capable of rehabbing again. I don't even know when rehabbing turned into a passion for me. I know to this day I can walk the isles of Home Depot or Lowes until I lose track of time. I lose myself imagining all the old things I can make new within the isles full of supplies. I have since hung my rehab hat up for a while but will certainly pick it up again soon.

I met many good people who are great at their skills and just as passionate about their jobs as I was about getting the work done. When you surround yourself with passionate people of similar interests and goals, you often find yourself doing something extraordinary. I happened upon a great realtor who is phenomenal in his job when my then-husband and I decided on selling one of our rental properties. I'm waiting patiently to come across the fixer-upper that is waiting for me to get my hands on to spruce back to life. Rehabbing was rewarding and exciting for me even though it didn't start as a dream or even anything I planned to be a part of, yet I became passionate about it. Even as I write this, I dream of re-entering the real estate market and flipping houses again. Little did I know the real estate allowed me to create another financial income that would catapult me to my salon dream.

I had to be around twelve years old when I drew a picture of a beauty salon I wanted to own in the future. I have been caring for hair for almost as long as I can remember. It was my first passion, and I still provide hair care for a few loyal clients to this day. I started off cutting and styling my dolls and Cabbage Patches; then, I started styling my own hair. I could do finger waves, twists, French rolls, spiral sets, and all sorts of creative styles on myself.

From there, I was actually styling my mom's hair with finger waves and French rolls, to roller sets and flat irons. I even styled my older sister's hair for her graduation pictures. My styles looked so nice that several people in my church started requesting me for their children's shampoo and styles. I was making good pocket change for my age between twelve and sixteen. I charged $5.00 for shampoo and sets, $15 for relaxers, and $5.00 for trims. I at that time thought this was a steal since I was using the client's electricity and water by going to their homes. I only used my styling supplies because I had preferences. The client purchased their own relaxer if needed, and I would apply it safely for them. My mom would carpool me from house to house with me lugging all my supplies along. I would carry my gold-n-hot hooded dryer, shampoos, conditioner, hair sprays, and all sorts of supplies to complete my customer needs.

I continued to style hair throughout my teens, enrolling in the cosmetology program in high school. I owe my mom many thanks for all the ways she helped support me in making money and earning my cosmetology license. After completing the cosmetology program, I went to State Board in 1998. When something happened beyond my control, my mom was with me that prevented me from taking the board test. It was the lack of proper identification from my model. Of course, it wasn't my model's fault that I didn't ensure proper identification before we set off, but I was devastated. Through my tears and snobs, I heard my mom go up to the window and tell the state board that she would be my model.

She gave them identification and started filling out the paperwork. The next thing I knew, they called us back to the window and said she couldn't be my model because she had a cosmetology license, although inactive from about twenty years ago. Neither of us could understand why such an old expired license mattered. The fact was state board would not allow it, for obvious reasons I see now, but I was so disappointed because I was so ready and excited to take the test.

After that didn't work out, I saw my mom through the glass windows, out on the front sidewalk, stopping passers-by. She was offering to pay them one hundred dollars to be my model for state board testing. Back then, for our family of five children, I knew that a hundred dollars was a lot of money for her to dish out. We almost had a taker until she found out the test would be several hours long. No one told me that I would be lucky enough or blessed, whichever way you see it, to experience such mother's love and belief in me shown in her actions. Tried as she did, we weren't able to find an alternate model for the test.

Both the model and myself were in tears for a while before finally calming down. I rescheduled and took the state board exam a month or two later, passing seven of the nine parts. I had to return a few weeks later to retake the two parts again, but I passed the second time with "flying colors" and received my cosmetology license. My mom was so proud of me. I was proud of myself too. This lesson taught me a few things: to be triple prepared, don't let a setback stop forward movement, and allow for a little more time and backup plans when setting out for a goal. I was getting a little bit closer to my dreams with everything I was accomplishing.

After I passed state board testing, I started working as a licensed cosmetologist in the salon of a woman who attended my church. I was in such bliss. I hardly had any clients to start with; I learned a lot from watching the women working in that salon. A lot happened over the next several years, like moving out of mom's house, college, marriage, childbirth, and many of life's other journeys. I worked at a tanning salon, a salon manager in a family hair care salon, and other salon retail positions that gave me a vast knowledge of the salon business's management. After all my combined experiences and the extra income from the rental properties, I started playing around with the idea of purchasing salon furniture. I didn't want to take out a loan after pricing salon equipment and seeing how expensive it was. I didn't know what kind of furniture I might find gently used, which didn't stop me from starting my search.

I started to look for salon equipment in 2009 seriously. I was looking online one day and saw that there would be an upcoming auction for this beautiful Koken salon furniture I absolutely fell in love with. My then-husband and I went to the specified place advertised only to be the only two people to show up for the auction. The auctioneer was like, "name your price for the furniture you want." I ended up getting practically brand new four full-sized styling stations with mirrors, three shampoo stations, and two retail shelves for $750. I was shocked and delighted, to say the least. The previous salon owner had purchased these seven feet Koken stations and went out of business shortly after. The auctioneer said the building owner had already re-rented the space and wanted the salon furniture out immediately, and was trying to recoup some of his losses. I knew then and there that the equipment was my blessing catered just for me. We rented a U-Haul, got some help, and moved all of the salon furniture to our home garage the very next day. I still was in disbelief of the sheer size and "deal of a lifetime" price I'd gotten for all the salon furniture. It sat in my garage for eight to nine months while looking for a location to open my business. When I finally found the space, it was worth the wait because the salon furniture fit in there so perfectly! I thought the experience of seeing my dream come to reality was one of the most extraordinary events of my life, and I will never forget the feeling I had. I was able to find all of my salon furniture for about two-thousand dollars. The way that those opportunities lined up for me at that exact time is how I knew it was meant to be.

The year was 2011 when I opened my Beauty Salon in Reynoldsburg, Ohio. My dream I had been dreaming since I was twelve years old came true. It didn't come without hard work, sacrifice, dedication, planning, and determination. I was willing to commit to whatever was needed to see my dream become a reality. Opening day was everything I had imagined with: Koken styling station, matching styling chairs, identical shampoo bowls, retail shelves, tile flooring, and the exact ambiance I was hoping to achieve. I was blessed to open the salon without any debt for salon furniture or supplies. Everything was all paid in full, so I began to build the business. During my college business classes, I learned it would take three to five years to build it well, so I knew the road ahead wouldn't be an easy one, but I was up for the challenge. In addition to opening the business, I also worked a full-time job and raised my toddler son with my husband. He had helped me significantly during the business launch. I focused on accomplishing my goal of self-employment and couldn't have done it without his support.

The business launch went well; I'd advertised to find a few cosmetologists to work with and was looking forward to filling the available booths. I helped support my household by keeping my full-time job during my first year of operating the business. At that time, my husband and I owned several rental properties to support our household and any business needs. My full-time job required me to arrive there at 6:30 am every morning. From there, I went directly to the salon opening about 3 or 4 o'clock each day until I found independent contractors that started in the morning. Sometimes I styled clients' hair until 9 or 10 at night. I kept up with those hours for the first year of business. During that first year, I found a couple of independent contractors who fit into the business well. They were in the salon working most mornings while I was at my full-time job. I won't forget how they helped and was a major part of me being able to fulfill my dream. After my clientele was building up, I decided to leave my full-time job to focus 100% on the business.

My business allowed me to make connections with awesome stylists, clients, people and utilize skills that I learned over my work and educational experiences. Owning and operating the day-to-day business gave me first-hand experience of how hard people work to succeed in their dreams. I have a greater understanding of what it takes to build a salon business successfully. I finalized every decision to add to or re-arrange the business. I was responsible for the reputation of my business and its growth. So I had to choose stylists who would represent me and my business well. Some sacrifices like less sleep, longer hours, and cutting back on my spending is what I had to do. Every day I turned the key to open the doors to my own business was worth every second of self-sacrifice.

Several jobs led me up to the point where I would be ready to launch my business. It took, for example, me working in a retail beauty salon as a manager gaining knowledge such as ordering supplies, accounting methods, interviewing potential stylists, and more to gain the experience I needed to start and operate the business. I started my business for several reasons: I wanted to be in control of my working hours, control my earnings as much as I could, have freedom from supervisors or managers, and also the tax breaks. I had been passionate about the arena of hair for so long. I styled numerous heads of hair for weddings, proms, and other important events. I've attended hair shows to stay abreast of industry trends and fashions as well as taking classes to enhance my skill. Uncle Sam was taking his due right off the top, and I wanted to be able to make deductions every year rather than have taxes automatically taken.

The end of year two was fast approaching; I used less money from our rental properties for the salon expenses' and was feeling good about my business survival. All of my booths were rented out, we were getting walk-ins and referrals, and business was feeling comfortable. I was excited when I reached the end of year three; I'd survived the first three years in business. The business income went from a net loss in year one to a much smaller net loss in year two, then I broke even in year three, and the fourth a net profit. I was over the moon that I finally made money in the fourth year and had a great positive outlook. This may not sound attractive for some; even so, it's the reality of the first few years of business. Had I not been sidetracked with the home renovations a few years earlier, I couldn't have established a second income to cushion my business and home expenses. I was willing to work another job to help supplement the income I was not bringing home. Few businesses turn profits within the first year, so congratulations for the ones that do. I was so pleased that I had moved from the E quadrant (employee) to the S quadrant (self-employed). I felt I was on my way to my goal of achieving the B quadrant (business owner). I had independent contractors who could work in the salon without me having to be inside the salon.

Just when business was looking great during that fourth year, I saw a trend of clients coming into the salon and asking for styles they'd seen on YouTube. After a while, I saw a decrease in new clients coming into the salon. I also noticed a decline in customers pointing in magazines instead they started pulling up apps or online pictures. Around this time, I saw the YouTube era of how to do your hair exploding. I should've known then that I needed to adjust my business practices.

The added stress of business decline to my failing marriage I wasn't ready to face proved to be too much. All I was focused on at the time is that my business thrived off of a lot of people who did not know how to care for or style their hair. There were tons of people that had to look professionally groomed for work, graduations, weddings, and other celebrations. Then seeming out thin air, hundreds if not thousands of YouTube videos showed step-by-step how to care for and style your hair. Both professionally licensed and unlicensed people gave very good instructions on how to do the styles and techniques I learned in school or picked up creatively throughout my hair career. Those videos boosted creativity for those at home who didn't normally do their hairstyling, especially the teens who usually got their unique and creative styles from the salon.

Not all of my normal clients were coming to the salon as often as usually did. Some would have longer periods of visits because they'd only schedule chemical services instead of the usual shampoo and styles. The decline in my business happened right when it should've been steadily increasing with the positive reputation I was building alongside other amazing stylists that worked with me. Just as I was living my dreams and getting to see the business prosper, life gave me lemons.

It was a complete jab in the dark when it came to figuring out how to fix my marriage and business. I knew I wanted to keep the business and adjust to the changing markets, but I also thought I couldn't do it independently. All of the practical resources during the course work I was able to apply to my business directly didn't help

139

with a broken heart. During college, I heard a lot of quotes being used like, "life is what you make it," "there's only one way to go from the bottom," or "when life gives you lemons, make lemonade." Well, what if I don't like lemonade? The truth is there are thousands of life quotes, motivational creeds, life coaches, and hundreds of other resources available for the masses. The trick that worked for me was to find the one or few that can apply to my life.

Life continues to teach me my plans don't always turn out the way I planned because if they had, I'd still be happily married to the man I once said my vows with. Sometimes the goals and plans I have feels impossible when I'm in the thick of it. But even if it takes a little longer to accomplish, if my mind is made up, no matter how rough things get, I can finish what I set out to. At the time, I didn't have enough energy to fight through solutions to keep the business on top and seemingly failing marriage. After going back and forth with myself, I sold my business while it was profitable to focus on myself, make decisions about my marriage, and rental properties.

In hindsight, I should have been able to adjust my business practices to change with the climate. I should've sold more retail products that the customers were using and had a more online presence. I could've even uploaded videos of what my stylists and I were doing to rouse interest, only then I didn't understand how valuable social media was to business. Plus, I wasn't interested in technology all that much, wasn't motivated in taking classes regardless of the fact that I had to learn it eventually.

That fourth year I know now was a time to celebrate; I instead chose to sell the business while I was in the green. That certainly wasn't the lemonade I wanted, but it was the decision I made at the time. I would now recommend that if you're a business struggling to stay on top, network with your other local business owners. See if you can trade or sell each other products and services. Some may even be willing to share what aspect of their business is working well. It is vital to share your strengths and weaknesses with other businesses so that you can find a way to thrive in stressful markets. There has to be some service or product you can offer your customers that they don't know they want or need. Or maybe even something that they already use but will be willing to give you the business purchasing online or storefront. One important thing my experience has taught me is to see each experience as a lesson. Each lesson has allowed growth and not a failure because I will know the smoother road to take next time.

In business, I have to know how to shift my practices to the end customer's needs and wants to succeed and thrive with market changes. I didn't have the level of support or mental energy I needed, although having my business for the short time I did has taught me all the better-learned things first-hand. We're currently seeing and experiencing unprecedented changes in the way business is done all over the world. I hope this helps others to push through to accomplish their business goals and dreams. I'm a perfect example of anyone being able to achieve whatever your dreams may be. Mine does not end here, there's more ahead, and I can hardly wait to continue my journey.

So my advice when it comes to business would be, if some bank, financial institution, or leaseholder says *"No,"* that's when you define the *"Yes"* yourself. Never stop because you can't get a loan or don't have enough money. Find a way to barter, bargain, or network with people who have the means. There could be someone who has the means only, not the time, so partner with them. Get them interested in your goals without giving your whole business plan and ideas away. Remember that you have a lot to offer even if you can't get a loan. You have the business plan and vision along with the research you've done to prove the concept. Be sure to do plenty of research on location, 3-5-year expense report, potential problems, and how you want to structure your company. If you hit a wall, educate yourself for free until things turn around.

The library and all of its resources, including the wonderful people who work there, are full of knowledge just waiting to be obtained. The library is where I read many self-help, financial, autobiographies, and many more books for free. It may take a while to sift through the methods and advice that works for you, but the journey is worthwhile. You can find a "how-to" book on practically any subject at the library. So take advantage of it because you never know what good information, resources, tools, or direction you can obtain just by opening a book. You can become knowledgeable about your craft or business, and the library is a great starting point as a free resource.

Don't stop there; join a forum, podcast, or another group to gain information and contacts. The more knowledge you have by surrounding yourself with like-minded people, the better off you'll be when the stars align for you. I believe that the best place to be is in the presence of the people who are already doing what you want to achieve to soak up the practices that can help your dream become a reality, just as mine did. If it can happen for me, I know it will work for you too.

Chapter 13

Will the real me please stand out?

I have been directed to follow the rules for most of my life, be good, be myself, be honest, don't lie, go to church, or do this and don't do that. When I look in the mirror, what do I even see? Is the real me looking back or everything I was made to be? Since the time I was very young, I've had this deep look in my eyes that penetrated everything I looked upon. I don't just look at people or things but seem to look past their exteriors and feel their vibes on the inside. I've been often told that I speak and listen with my eyes.

Once during a conversation with my pre-marital counselor, he told me I listened intently with my eyes. At times I find myself looking into someone's eyes as they're talking, seeming to feel what is said instead of just listening. At other times, I appear to be intently listening only I'm far away in my thoughts of an observation I've made about them. Some of those thoughts would be forming opinions on the things I really want to say but hold back in fear of offending a people's feelings. At other times, I'm concentrating on their hair or trying to remember what I want to say in response to what is being said. Sometimes it's so hard for me not to interrupt and put my opinion in because I know I'll forget by the time the person finishes talking. Sometimes I ask myself, does this person just want to vent, or do they want my advice? I always thought it was important to look a person in the eyes when conversing to show that they have my attention. So many rules, laws, and traditions have always seemed so questionable from my view. Why did I have to follow the rules? I prefer to dance to the beat of my own drum. I prefer to be a part of the crowd, more so blending in, not the one with all the attention. I can't help but think sometimes I'm supposed to stand out in a good way. I stood out in a way all through my school-age years because I was different; quiet, very aware, observing, and never missing anything going on around me. Being Christian, I tried to interact positively with people, portray Christian love, and treat people well. I don't always succeed, which is why I understand the passage, "when I would do good, evil is forever present with me." (Romans 7:21) I stand out in other circles because of my entrepreneurial mind and thinking. I'm constantly thinking of ways to get back to my business endeavors. The real me is definitely looking back when I look in the mirror.

The real me has stood out throughout my whole life when I think about it. Even after I left my home city and church, I still clung to some foundational truths that I learned growing up. I've always been able to dress however I felt comfortable, regardless of the current fashion trend. I can't claim that I've ever been a trendsetter but have certainly tried to be presentable. Not sure about fashionable!

Throughout my school-aged years, including later in life, people who meet my mother always told her what a sweet or lovely daughter she has. I think that my mother has taught me how to carry myself well, whether at home or in public places. I have gotten so used to being polite, mannerable, and appropriately behaved at work and in public places; sweet has become second nature for me. When I'm in my own home or my family's homes, it's easy for me to shed all the etiquette and say what I feel without censoring per se. I'm not sure how much my family appreciates it, but they see me in my truest form the most. I am a sweet, light-hearted person, but I'm also fierce, straightforward, and bold when I need to be.

Most people I interact with daily only see part of who I am, but those closest to me, like family or close friends, get to see the good and the imperfect parts of me. The imperfections I see get me to want to do better. Because of those realities, I see the need to improve myself daily and the boldness gives me the fierceness to take me places I'd never thought I would've gone.

The real me had no idea how much I craved information, education, and knowledge before reading the *Rich Dad Poor Dad* book. I've always equated more money to working longer hours. I thought working overtime or getting an extra job was the answer to making more money for me. After I read the book, I knew finding a way for my money to work for me was the long-term answer. That's not something taught in every college course; it's different from stocks and bonds or retirement plans. I didn't just apply the techniques I learned and read about overnight. I had to be intentional with the work experience I gained to get closer to where I wanted to be.

I've been employed as janitor assistant, banquet server, waitress, cashier, cosmetologist, production associate, quality control, self-employed, rental properties owner, special education assistant, and a few more titles. I've got to say that each job has prepared me for my journey because I wouldn't have had the necessary tools to reach my business goals without them. The combined experiences have made me realize how I can impact society in my way. I've been able to take away what works well at each of my employment places and use it at others.

One takeaway was the superior way that mission was carried out, ensuring that in the end, the customer received the highest quality product and not letting the customer always be right. Another takeaway was company expectations, from the top executive to the floor sweeper, to be treated fairly and kindly. From my first job, I loved having my own money, not necessarily the money itself. I knew money would come, and money would go, but as long as I knew how to make it, I'd be ahead of a few others. Some of the amounts that I have earned wouldn't be much for some or significant to others, but I earned it. The dollars I earned went a long way in my teens, and I've always figured a way to make them stretch as an adult, too, spending on things that had value to me.

I always am honest with myself, being responsible for my well-being, and always organizing and prioritizing my life for my future journey. There have been times when I made what I would call a significant amount of money and times when I lived paycheck to paycheck. The financial foundation I got from my mother allowed me to be efficient in both. I have found no matter if I have a little money or a lot to be determined to be happy in either.

I found that my attitude in each unpleasant situation makes even undesirable situations more manageable, which makes a huge difference in my out-look. Just because I was living paycheck to paycheck for a time didn't mean I couldn't be happy. After all, almost every circumstance in life is temporary. Few things in life are guaranteed aside from change, life, and death. Some would include taxes.

Nobody told me: when you have a setback, use it as a lesson, not a failure. Some say, "I take one step forward only to take two steps backward." I've learned to view those two steps back differently. Instead, here is the way I think of those two steps back: it is as a way for me to be behind my obstacle or opposition so that I have a better view to analyze what's going on more efficiently. I have the vantage point of seeing moves made clear to plan the best way to attack and overcome them. My opposition is no longer behind me to catch me by surprise; I can see or predict what's lies ahead now. I may not have realized it, but the setback sets me up with the knowledge to expect obstacles and opposition and prepare for them when they do come. Instead of implementing a countermeasure afterward, I can implement a plan for when temporary setbacks happen.

So think of life's challenges that way, and you'll always see those minor or major setbacks as opportunities. This will change your whole attitude, allowing you to handle the situation with a much clearer head and focus. I use this thought process sometimes, asking myself what I did wrong. It helps me in business and personal situations when I have to take a hard look at things.

Life is extraordinary whether you have all your needs met or are looking for ways to fill all your needs. One major thing I think I almost have mastered is a quote that I heard a long time ago, "circumstances don't control my happiness; happiness controls my circumstances." When you decide to be happy even though your circumstances aren't where you want them to be, you're telling yourself that it's ok that life has its ups and downs. It's how you face them that allows you to soar through and above them. For example, if I paid all my living expenses and utilities and didn't have a dime left until the next payday, I could still be happy because I didn't owe anybody. Not only can I appreciate life's other gifts like walking through the park, calling up a friend to catch up, taking a long hot bath to relax, or just looking up at the sky and enjoying the earthly beauty. I can be thankful that I can pay all my bills because there are people with no home, car, or means to do just that.

A few years ago, I was staring in the mirror, asking myself could I travel comfortably alone to vacation and enjoy my own company. I realized right away that yes, I could travel solo yet safely if I took certain measures to ensure my well-being. So I went to New Orleans, Louisiana, to attend the Essence festival that year in 2017. Some may think it's dangerous to vacation alone, but I felt it was both adventurous and confidence-building.

I wanted to go somewhere to get away for a while, and when I saw all that the festival had to offer, I knew I wanted to attend. I didn't start off planning to go by myself yet; that's how it ended up. Sometimes I feel like I have to just go for it no matter if I have to enjoy my own company, by the way, which is very nice. After all, I love myself and want to treat myself now and again. Many things that I have done and experienced made this trip seem like a walk in the park. When my flight arrived in New Orleans, I got a transportation service to drop me off a couple of blocks from my hotel, check-in, change and put my luggage down to freshen up, and off I went to explore. I remember the southern heat hitting me like a slap in the face. I hadn't felt any humidity even close other than visiting Miami, Florida, a few years earlier.

Over the next five days that I stayed in New Orleans, I took a different approach than some. I wanted to see the real people of New Orleans and all the places that weren't so pretty or touristy. Instead of booking tours, I took the city buses from one end of the city to another, traveling as far north, south, east, and west as they would take me.

While I traveled, I observed the everyday people going and coming to-and-from work, talked with the bus drivers about the city, and took pictures of inner-city neighborhoods. I saw that most of the streets and people weren't that different from my community, aside from the southern accents. It was moving to see how high some of the old water lines from hurricane Katrina still stained some homes and businesses. I was grateful that I have never lived below sea level or in a state prone to hurricanes or natural disasters. I was able to see how other homes were rebuilt on higher foundations to avoid water damage from incoming storms. It showed that the people have persevered amid adversity and still love their city. It also encouraged me to face adversity with calm and reassured me that working together brings about greater results than working alone. I had to look in the mirror each morning as I readied myself for another adventurous day, feeling more and more confident in myself, who I was, and where my path was taking me.

While in New Orleans, I also enjoyed all that Bourbon Street had to offer. It was amazing how lively it was with loud music, great food, lots of shopping, colorful people, attire, and drinks that seemed to flow all day long. After spending my days at the convention center in exhibit halls, panel discussions, and star gazing at actors and actresses, I often went out to do more exploring in the city. The upside to me vacationing on my own is that I didn't have to coordinate with another person on where I went, how long I stayed, how to divide the days, or anything of the such. It was freeing not to make sure my traveling partner wanted to do all the same things as me or go to all the same places. I enjoyed nightly concerts hearing music from awesome artists, who came along with the Essence ticket I bought. Plus, I saved a bundle by not using costly transportation services. I will vacation solo again because my experience here showed me how much I enjoy my own company.

I tried to think back during my flight back home and ask myself, have I dreamed of getting married? I don't think that I ever have. I had a lot of time to reflect on my failed marriage and the events or causes that led to the failure. It was an adventure when I went off to college, got my first apartment solo, bought my first house renovation, said "I do," and birthed my son. I may've thought that marriage would be my best adventure, and since I thought it would last a lifetime, it interrupted my plans when it didn't. I can easily remember my beauty salon dreams and being in a relationship, but not necessarily marriage.

Marriage is what was expected of me; I had been taught growing up most of my life that if you had a sexual partner, you should marry them. Hearing those teachings over and over during those Sunday services, Wednesday bible classes, and Friday saints' meetings to do so, had me giving more than a few nudges to Mr. Fine to marry me. I thought it would help me feel I was in right standing with my religious teachings. I thought being married would solve the nagging reminder that I was not living according to those teachings, and it did, for a while. I jumped into marriage with two feet, thinking that mine would unfold just like a fairytale. The only problem was, just like anything else new, the hype wore off, and I was left with chasing that emotional high of love I felt in the beginning. It seemed towards the end we didn't understand one another's needs and didn't make the conscious choice to love each other.

When I looked at myself during those almost ten years of being married, I was used to having an out if things didn't work out for me. Like the other things in my life like jobs, friendships, or home base, it was routine for me to want just to change when I wasn't happy. If a job wasn't everything I wanted it to be, I got a new one. If a friendship wasn't the way I thought it should be, I ended it. I thought this was the way I was supposed to keep control of what I wanted my life to look like. I wasn't supposed to treat my marriage that way, or any relationship for that matter. Every time I look in the mirror, I learn more about my shortcomings. I learn from reflections of my past, and I see the present as an opportunity to be more successful on my journey.

When I look in the mirror now, I see my flaws and have learned to be okay with them. I see forgiveness for myself and others. I see a woman who has grown, a beautiful and confident person looking back, and a woman who is quick to apologize. I have been a person for most of my life that has hated apologizing. To say I was sorry felt like it wouldn't change what I had already said or done. Most of the time, whatever the offense was, I intended for it to offend. That's why I saw apologies as useless because I felt I could not unhurt a person once the wrong was said or done as sorry is for remorse.

Now, more than ever, I try to right my wrongs as quickly as possible, which notes extreme growth for me. It's not so much that I would say I liked admitting I was wrong, but doing so made me feel vulnerable and weak. I've seen first-hand only in the recent years of my life that not only saying but expressing apologies are necessary to help others heal, forgive, and get closure.

Apologies are necessary to allow myself to feel the hurts I've caused in order not to make the same choice again. That is when I see myself growing and maturing when I change on the inside, and it's reflected by the words of my mouth and actions. So if you have to apologize to anybody, don't do so by words of your mouth alone. Let the apology be expressed by your actions also. Sometimes apologies need to be felt as well as said.

I also see my past in which I wish I would've spoken up to protect my siblings from mean kids. I don't know that as a child, I even could see that if I have spoken up, I could've made such an impact on the teasing my siblings endured. I wish I hadn't fought so much with my brothers growing up to try and get them to do what I told them to. I see why people say, "if I knew then what I know now," because it would've made a huge difference on a few decisions I made growing up. When my two brothers would pick on my little sister, I went right down to their rooms and called them out on it, even if it leads to a physical fight. If my older sister was using too much discipline on my younger sister, I went head to head with her to stop it. I just wish I had the same ferocity to protect my siblings against outside kids in what they said to them when we were in our teens. I wish I would've realized that I couldn't control everything around me.

After my parents split up when I was twelve, my mom worked a lot to provide for us. I felt the need to make sure everyone at home played their role while mom was out working. So, I took on the lead role in making sure everything at home was how it was supposed to be, even if it meant fighting my brothers or strong-arming my sister.

I wasn't a large child by any means, but I had presence when I meant to get something done. Fast forward to adulthood; I've been able to look in the mirror to see and analyze the few regrets that I have over my life, and thank God there aren't very many. The regrets that bother me the most have seemed to lie with decisions I made regarding my family directly.

One regret I have is that I didn't ask my grandad to walk me down the aisle once I knew my dad wasn't coming to my wedding. Whether the regret was something that I said or didn't say, did, or didn't do, I see now a different decision could've made all the difference. Only I can't go backward, just forward. Whatever revelation in your life that marks growth for you own it and move forward.

The reflection looking back at me in my mirror is also a mother, a daughter, a grand-daughter, a sister, a niece, a cousin, a friend, a provider, a home-maker, a strong, passionate, caring, two-folded, determined goal setting, goal-reaching, beautiful and uniquely made woman. When I look in the mirror, I see a fearless woman, resourceful, grateful, and so many other attributes I couldn't explain in just a few words. I want and need to achieve my purpose on this journey. I don't want to journey through life alone, but I want to grab hold of as many hands I can to take with me. I want to look to my right and my left and see my family, friends, and community soaring to high heights beside me.

I wish more people viewed life as so many journeys short and long. The situations or circumstances, good or bad, will hit our emotions in ways we don't always expect. We all have had to face that fork in the road to determine what path we take and what we make of it. When we choose our paths as individuals, we have to choose the ones that are strengthening our purposes. Only I'm in charge of the journey that I want to travel, just as you are in control of yours. I can no longer blame my mishaps or setbacks on lack of resources, lack of support, or know-how; neither can you. There are way too many opportunities available not to accomplish whatever our dreams are if we're willing to put in the hard work it takes.

When I'm connected with my inner self, there isn't anything that feels too hard. No matter how long it takes like writing this book. It took some discipline to turn the television off and dedicate some time to typing these words. I used to think I didn't have enough time for volunteering or group meetings and social circles; rather, I found that I make time for whatever is important to me. It takes so much discipline and purposeful planning to stay motivated and keep moving towards my goals. I have to visualize the end goal to keep a steady pace towards progress. So, that brings me to my next questions. Is it true when it's said you just have to have mind over matter? Well, often when I'm at the park jogging my ¾ mile, during that last ¼ my body feels like I can't make it. My mind is telling me to stop that I can't run another step. Only something won't let me quit because I know if I stop, I won't finish the distance I intended to complete. I certainly can attest to some difficult choices.

I had to make one choice in the past, choosing to leave an item at the mall so I wouldn't pull out my credit card to pay for it. For you, it may be choosing water instead of soda. I do know from experience if I make up my mind to do something, no matter the temptation, I can do it. I can reach my goals, no matter how long it takes. I have found, it takes visuals and daily checklists to get me motivated, keep myself motivated, and visually see the checklists shrinking.

We're all living in an age where people everywhere are craving information, craving ways for their lives to become more convenient, and want to spend money to achieve it. I hope that I can encourage a few people to look in their own mirrors and see all the possibilities they have. To look at themselves and be confident that their journeys have a purpose, meaning, and value, however the path twists and turns. I am here to serve, uplift, give love, and always push people who are in my life to soar because I feel I soar with you when you soar. I'm proud of where my journey has taken me thus far without any boasting. I know the mirror reflects everything I've been taught and experienced so far on my journey. That is what I see when I look in my mirror.

If my life is a gift, then I will freely give

I don't think anyone lies in bed at night as a child staring at the ceiling, wishing and dreaming of being poor their whole life, not finishing high school, or letting their church or religion dictate every corner of their personal life. All through my young adult years, I've dreamed of what lies ahead, wondering what my future can look like.

Days in which I could make conscious choices to position myself so that I could freely give others the same tenacity to achieve their dreams as I had. I'm constantly thinking of ways to continue to reach for the things I want out of my journey. There was a time I was feeling especially motivated and told myself, "Can't" is no longer allowed in my house. That was one of those times when I was going through some unforeseen difficulties and encouraged myself. I try to teach my son not to say he can't do something so that he will only find another way to "can." I think it's very important to teach children they can do whatever they dream of because if we do, they will find a way to make their ideas realities. It doesn't take much to see extraordinary people and things in the world all around us. I can look back and see extraordinary moments in my life that perhaps may have been missed by people not looking to find extraordinary things. I see ordinary people doing extraordinary things when others look the other way.

I was sitting in the park on a summer day and looked up at the clouds moving overhead and thought how extraordinary creation is. The vast blue sky overhead was covered with the most beautiful white clouds in various shapes and sizes. I just thought how amazing the Creator is for placing every cloud in the sky for its job to precipitate, condensate, and contribute to our climate.

One evening I was watching a nightly news story broadcasting a story of a complete stranger changing another complete strangers' life by giving them an organ needed for survival. This person wasn't even related to the person who needed the organ but felt compelled to donate anyway. That's extraordinary. If you watch closely, you'll see what I'm talking about exactly, catching something extraordinary happening around you.

I could go on and on about amazing people and amazing things. I encourage you to take some time to look around areas in your life. I'm sure you'll find some extraordinary things or people such as yourself or someone you know. What about that person who beyond addiction or arrest who has turned their life around and is guiding others by their personal story? What about the man or woman who are the first in their family to go to college? How about the executive or CEO who, beyond developmental disabilities, have defied the odds and started and excelled in their own company. The person who walked away from an accident, tragedy, or devastation and decided not to waste another single minute of life. The person living in Beverly Hills who grew up in the ghetto on government assistance. The boy who grew up on the south side of Chicago and became President of the United States. They all are extraordinary.

If extraordinary to you is rolling out of bed every morning putting one foot down, then the other to get yourself to start the day, you are extraordinary! If extraordinary for you is walking past the liquor store one more day, you are extraordinary! If extraordinary for you is paying your rent or mortgage, utilities, insurances, and still having leftover for groceries, you are extraordinary! However, you define your extraordinary, be proud of what you accomplish because it isn't every day that you find the extraordinary in your journey every day.

If nothing else, we're all connected by one thing, humanity. Whether you've come from humble beginnings like me or grew up in 10,000 square feet with personal cooks and chauffeurs, we're all reaching for something. Whether we've arrived or working on future ways to stay at the top, we can all give a little time or advice to help our counterparts succeed. I've learned to appreciate life lessons, joys, hardships, and flourishing. The hardships continue to help me become resourceful, the joys build me up to endure the hardships, and the flourishing pushes me to give myself to others.

I began writing this book because I thought to myself, "there have to be other people like me," maneuvering through life, wondering if they're getting it all right. The truth is I won't always get it right, neither will you. It's what actions and lessons we learn when we're wrong that counts the most. I asked myself, "what if I shared my story? In doing so, I hope that it has helped someone to make a few connections or get that "just clicked" feeling reference to a light bulb emotion. Would sharing my story help someone along their journey? I hope that it does and perhaps helps to leap you into your destiny, purpose, or dream. If I had to walk this journey all over again, there wouldn't be much I'd want to change because I am who I am because of all the things I've experienced along the way.

If it were not for the love my parents gave me as they raised me, along with the discipline and business sense I retained from them, I couldn't have dreamed all the dreams that I had and worked so hard to see them a reality. Without my marriage, I wouldn't have an incredibly light-hearted, easy-going, fun-laughing, curious-natured, and love-giving son. Not to mention the good times I had while joined to another soul for such a time as I experienced. If it weren't for my education, I wouldn't have been given the tools to spark my interest in all of the amazing things that have happened in my life. I certainly wouldn't have written this book if I had listened to my conscience about the sacrifice it would take to finish it. My strong roots have consistently, over the years, breathed strength, courage, protection, love, and faith into my life. I couldn't have been so successful without all the strength of my humble beginnings and so many intentionally placed people in my life to guide me. So if you have a parent, friend, or significant other pushing you in uncomfortable ways, it's because they see all the wonderful places you could go and things you could accomplish on your journey.

Nobody told me that I would look at my journey so far and see the roads that I've taken and the decisions I've made, surmount to so much courage to keep on pursuing more, giving more, and appreciating life. Nobody told me I couldn't be more than proud of what I've accomplished so far because of all the answers I found on my own. I will be more than generous with my knowledge, truth, and understanding. I will continue to give my time, love, and talent to my family and community.

I want people to know that you can find the extraordinary in your journey. I want people to realize; dreams really do come true for everyone, no matter where you come from. It doesn't matter your social-economic status; whether your parents set the bar high or not, set your own bar high. Be accountable for your actions. Even if someone told you that you couldn't do that, if you believe you can, that's all you need to start. Use your narrative as I have used mine to take responsibility for creating the path on your journey you envision, even if it's a path unfamiliar. Enjoy the adventure that it brings; you never know what connections you may make along the way. We live in an age where anything is possible; if you can dream it, you can achieve it, be sure to enjoy the journey along the way.

Author Contacts:

Email: Pleasantinvestments123@gmail.com

Website: Pleasantinvestments.com

Resource Page

This is a little something extra for those who want to start something but need a little direction of where to begin.

<u>Start a business</u>

https://www.sba.gov

https://www.ohiosos.gov/businesses/information-on-starting-and-maintaining-a-business/starting-a-business/

<u>Write a book (I found at my local library)</u>

The Nonfiction Book Publishing Plan: The professional guide to profitable self-publishing. Stephanie Chandler and Karl W. Palachuk 2018

How to self-Publish for under $100: The step-by-step handbook to publish your book without breaking the bank. Cinquanta Cox-Smith 2017

<u>Financial Help (Book, Audiobook, or CD)</u>

David Bach: Debt-Free for Life

Dave Ramsey: Financial Peace